What Others Are Saying

"The Diary of a Reluctant Atheist' is the living disproof of Richard Dawkins' charge that all believers are 'faith heads.' A dedicated atheist like the controversial new atheist himself, David Bock shows how a philosopher and a business man thinks through the meaning of life and pursues truth at whatever cost. A fascinating story, grippingly told, and an open invitation to all who are searching for what Socrates called an 'examined life.' Highly recommended."

Os Guinness, author *Long Journey Home*

"David Bock's narrative of his evolution from a committed atheist to a Christian believer is powerful and convincing. From Viennese churches to Oxford colleges, from academic conversations to a life-threatening health drama in the African bush, David's story is rich in detail and made more moving by the powerful love and spiritual partnership with his wife Pam. Whether you are a student, a business person, or just someone with the restless spirituality, you will find *The Diary of a Reluctant Atheist* a compelling read."

David Aikman, author *Great Souls, Jesus in Beijing,* and other books.

'The Universe is made of stories not of atoms,' poet Muriel Rukeyser famously proclaimed. Stories are how we make sense of the world and our place in it. But is there a story that is big enough to build our lives upon? That gives our lives ultimate meaning and purpose?

By sharing his journey from atheism to faith, author David Bock takes both believers and seekers on a pilgrimage that reveals that our lives can have greater meaning than we could ever possibly imagine.

The Reluctant Atheist helps us to discover the meaning of our individual stories – our identity, our purpose, our destiny – by ultimately helping us understand the big story, what has been called *'the greatest story ever told.'*

This book will inspire Christians, and is a perfect book for thoughtful seekers. I highly recommend it! "

Becky Manley Pippert, author *Out of the Salt Shaker,*
Hope Has Its Reasons, Live/Grow/Know

The Diary of A Reluctant Atheist

David Bock

ISBN: 0692515615
ISBN 13: 9780692515617

Table of contents

To Pam
Wife, Companion, Friend

Man does not create truth...
Rather, truth discloses itself to man when he perseveringly seeks it.

Karol Wojtyla, Polish Philosopher
(aka Pope John Paul II)

Preface

THE NEW ATHEISM IS ONE of the more interesting social trends of our time.

Atheism is growing in popularity as religious affiliation continues to decline, concepts of truth become more about personal preference, and religious fundamentalism in various parts of the world threatens freedom of conscience, tolerance and the hard-won social peace of a liberal democratic order.

If religion leads to intolerance, oppression and rule by autocrats enforced 'by the sword' that no one besides particular religious bigots find appealing, why wouldn't any sensible person choose to be an atheist?

At one time, I thought like this. Religion seemed to me to be an anachronism left over from a pre-scientific age. I could see all sorts of things I didn't like about religion and thought that it needed to be replaced by objective philosophical and scientific ways of thinking.

But then I went on a journey...

The purpose of the journey was to study philosophy in Europe. But it turned into a journey of discovery. Early on, I was challenged to think again about the Judeo-Christian worldview. The challenge wasn't so much philosophical as it was experiential and relational. I encountered a spiritual dimension to life – God, if you will – through a series of seemingly unconnected experiences that softened my atheism, opened my mind to the positive role that religion has played in Western culture and made it impossible for me to deny or ignore the yearning for transcendence that I now believe is common to all human beings.

A decade later, the journey culminated in a simple prayer over dinner with friends, with a life-changing transformation in my view of what we know and how we know it.

'So,' you might be asking, 'is this just another Christian conversion story? Why read it?'

I can think of three reasons.

First, I think it's an interesting story. But then, I'm biased. After all, it's *my* story.

To compensate for my bias, I've tried to tell it in an interesting way, in the form of diary that is faithful to what actually happened but retells the story in a more compressed way, sometimes bringing together events and conversations that happened over an extended period of time into a single encounter or conversation.

Second, intellectual transformations don't just happen.

They result from a *process* that takes time and may offer some strange twists and turns along the way. Going from atheism to faith (and vice versa) is a journey in its own right. If you're in process, on a journey yourself, you're likely to find the paths other people have taken to be helpful in discovering your own. Hopefully, my story with all its peculiarities might contribute to the unfolding of your own story, particularly if you're a younger person working your way through the transitions that people typically make from the world they grow up in to the world they choose for themselves

Third, in the end we all *choose* a worldview.

This is where I think the New Atheism (or the Old Atheism, for that matter) breaks down. However much atheists like to claim the moral high ground of reason, science and philosophy, atheism still involves a choice of how to see reality and how to interpret the world. Ultimately, neither science nor social criticism forces anything on us when it comes to worldview. We still choose it, and the key to a good life is to start with a good worldview.

I hope you'll walk with me on this journey, maybe for only a few pages, but maybe long enough to join me for dinner with my friends.

Prologue

PAM AND I ARE IN the car on our way to a cocktail party at some friends' house in Virginia. As we head down the hill from our neighborhood to Mass Avenue, Pam asks, *apropos* of nothing,

"What do you think about this God business?"

For some reason, I don't find the question surprising or out of place. I know Pam has been reading books on Christianity for the last few weeks. A decade ago, Pam's interest in religion would have created enormous stress in our relationship, but I guess I'm now in the category of 'mellowed' or 'reluctant' atheist. Religion is still not my thing, but now I can be at least tolerant if not mildly supportive of my wife's interest in the topic.

To complicate things a bit more, Pam's recent interest resulted from *my* getting into a religious discussion with one of my fellow McKinsey associates. That led to a budding friendship with Scott and his wife Ruth – who has been supplying Pam with her reading material. So, I guess I need to go along for the ride, as they say.

This evening, however, the phrase 'this God business' triggers a peculiar sort of connection between my intense study of philosophy during my hardline atheist days and some recent work on analysis of risk in capital investment decisions.

I come up with a one-sentence reply to Pam's question.

"I think the downside risks of not believing are rather large."

This off the cuff, flippant answer seems to satisfy Pam. Or, maybe it just stops a conversation before it can get started.

We drive up Mass Avenue to Westmoreland Circle, then down Dalecarlia Boulevard towards Chain Bridge. Pam is quiet, I assume lost in her own thoughts, and I begin unpacking the downside risk comment in my head.

I realize that the 'God business' for me has always been one of facts, logic and necessity.

Is belief in God necessary to explain the world around us?

Are religious convictions true based on verifiable evidence?

What is the syllogism whose conclusion is: 'Therefore, God exists'?

I have never found a convincing, i.e., non-disprovable, philosophical argument for the existence of God. In the philosophical paradigm, religious belief can never be more than a leap of faith, a willful suspension of the ground rules of rationality.

What surprises me this evening is how a *business* concept about decisions under conditions of uncertainty might play into this journey of understanding.

If I have learned anything at McKinsey & Company, it is the importance of fact-based decision making. The art of management is to be both
fact-based *and* decisive. You don't have the luxury of infinite time or resources, particularly in major capital investments. So you gather enough
information to reduce risk to acceptable levels and analyze the distribution
of possible outcomes – the 'upside' and the 'downside'.

Then you make a decision.

As we cross the Potomac River, my mind drifts back to Africa and a
book I read at the time about a religious conversion. I remember something
about not being able to come to Christianity through the intellect. You have
to *experience* Christ and then the intellect follows. Or something like that.

For a moment, the thought enters my head that 'maybe you just need
to make a decision', but I quickly dismiss it. Religion is *not* business, it is
not a matter of facts but of opinion, self-deception, myth, superstition, etc.
The evidence just isn't there.

At the same time, like scenes in a movie, a series of past encounters
and conversations about religion, philosophy, economics, politics and 'the
meaning and purpose of life' begin to roll through my memory.

I remember a brief but sharp conversation with a Catholic priest in Salt
Lake City, getting trapped into a Vespers service in a monastery in Germany,
hitting the wall in my search for meaning in Vienna, meeting Pam, becoming a father, coming way too close to dying in the plains of Africa.

So, what *do* I think about this 'God business' that once preoccupied
me so negatively as an atheist but also more positively in my search for
ultimate meaning and truth? Is this intellectual journey still underway?
Does it have a destination? If so, what?

I thought I had put this search for meaning behind me. But once again (thanks to my wife) the big existential questions are forcing themselves to the surface. What's the upside of religious experience? Equally important, what's the downside of my lingering, somewhat reluctant atheism?

Part One

CHAPTER 1

Ambush in Mormon Territory

Early December, Salt Lake City

I GOT AMBUSHED TODAY. INTELLECTUALLY, that is.

The day started fine. It's one of those warm winter days in Utah, bright sun and clear blue skies. I'm spending another Saturday driving from place to place in the Salt Lake Valley delivering special events orders for the local Coca-Cola bottler. While I would rather be busting trails in the fresh powder at Alta, the job pays the college bills, and my skiing has to fit in with work and studying.

The current delivery is to a Catholic church near the downtown business district. The dispatcher's instructions were to stop at the Rectory and ask someone to show me where to deliver the Coke and other drinks for the parish holiday event.

I haven't spent a lot of time around Catholic churches (none, to be precise), and I'm not quite sure what to expect.

I find what I imagine to be the Rectory, park my truck, walk up the steps and ring the doorbell. A priest opens the door, looks at me with puzzlement for a moment, then says, "Oh, yes. Just park over by that door. I'll get the keys and be right with you."

The priest gestures in the general direction of a side door on the church hall, and disappears back into the Rectory.

I recognize that the priest is not being abrupt, just efficient. It isn't hard for him to figure out why I rang the bell at the Rectory. I'm dressed in a white uniform with green pinstripes that makes me look a bit like a New York Yankee with an "It's the Real Thing" badge on my chest, and I'm driving a big truck with a Coca-Cola logo on it.

The priest is in his own version of a uniform – black suit, clerical collar, Crucifix around his neck. He's in his early 30s, medium height, wearing glasses, good looking, muscular – the sort of person Central Casting would send if you asked for someone to play the priest in an Italian mob movie.

St. Patrick's is a substantial but fairly plain building, made of brick and stucco assembled according to a loosely applied mission architecture design, and looking a little like the Alamo. As I move the truck, it occurs to me that the church could also be called '*Fort* St. Patrick.' Salt Lake City may be the most diverse part of Utah, but the Mormons still run the place. From a Catholic perspective, St. Patrick's is definitely in the middle of 'Mormon Territory'.

I start unloading the cases of fizzy water in the order, stacking them on the ground ready to be wheeled into the church. 'Damn,' I think. 'I bet I'm going to have to haul this stuff down into the basement.' The priest arrives, unlocks the door, flips on a light and sure enough, there's the flight of stairs down to the basement. The priest disappears again. A few minutes later, as I'm emerging from the basement sweaty and somewhat out of breath, he reappears.

"So what's a nice Mormon boy like you doing delivering Coca-Cola?" he asks.

The question is delivered in a friendly, teasing tone, and I take it as a fairly clever way to get a conversation started about morals and the role of religious belief.

For many years, the Mormon Church has lumped Coca-Cola in the category of *Strong Drink*, along with coffee, tea, whiskey and the like, all things Mormons are supposed to avoid. The priest thinks he's putting me on the spot with his question, based on a guess that I'm part of the vast Mormon tribe occupying the Salt Lake Valley.

My goal is to duck the conversation, get back in my truck and get on with a pleasant morning's work.

"I'm not a Mormon," I reply, pulling a few more cases off the truck.

"So what are you? Lutheran? Methodist?"

The priest has figured out that I'm definitely not Catholic, given my complete lack of proper etiquette in dealing with priests. What he doesn't know is that he is the first Catholic priest I have ever had a conversation with, and this is first time I have gotten near a Catholic church – and then only by the service entrance.

I stop stacking cases, and look at the priest.

"I'm an atheist."

A puzzled look crosses his face for a moment.

"You mean, you don't believe in God at all?"

"Yup, that's what the term implies."

I sense that he's busy shifting gears, having expected a debate about the *One True Church*, or possibly not having had much experience with outright atheists in Salt Lake City. I feel a bit sorry for him but also a bit self-satisfied. I grab the hand-truck and wheel another load down the basement stairs.

When I emerge, even sweatier and again a bit out of breath, the priest is reloaded, saddled up and ready for me. He smiles.

"You realize, don't you, that God exists whether you believe in him or not? Everything around us is created by him, including you."

He sweeps his arm across the vacant parking lot.

"He is the necessary first cause of all things, without which there would be nothing."

I'm familiar with the argument. What the priest doesn't know is that I'm not just a Coca-Cola delivery guy but also a philosophy student who is fully committed to an atheist – and hence anti-clerical – worldview.

I fold my arms across my chest, obscuring the 'It's the Real Thing' badge and give the priest a smug over-the-sunglasses look.

"You know, I don't really buy the god-of-the-gaps argument. The universe is just there, a product of the Big Bang. History shows that science has progressively pushed back religion as an explanation of anything. Purpose is a human invention and ascribing purpose to the universe is a form of self-deception."

Having delivered this monologue, I head off to the basement again without waiting for a reply.

When I return to the truck, the priest is still standing there, pensively, and ready to continue the conversation. I throw the handcart into a side bin in the truck and give the priest a receipt to sign. He scribbles his name at the bottom and hands the receipt back to me.

"I don't think you really understand the Christian view of God," he says, hoping to take our discussion forward.

I put the receipt in my deliveryman's wallet and stuff it in a pin-striped back pocket. I look at him and load the Big Arrow in the Big Bow.

"To me, the Christian concept of God is a bundle of contradictions. If he's supposed to be running the universe in a good way, he's either incredibly incompetent or some weird mixture of good and evil. I can't believe in a God who is supposedly good, omniscient, omnipresent, omnipotent, omni-whatever and still a bungler who causes so much human and animal suffering. That kind of a God I don't need.

"In any event, even if there were a God, I wouldn't want him in my life. I intend to take responsibility for myself and really don't see the need for the crutch of religion."

The priest seems to rock back on his heels for a moment.

"But that's *pride*," he replies.

He says it forcefully, with a bit of fire in his eyes, as if he were rebuking a member of his parish. The playful teasing and repartee are suddenly gone. At the same time, I feel the force of his concern. The rebuke is intended to make me think.

We stand facing each other in the parking lot for a long moment. Thanks to a freshman humanities course, I'm pretty aware of what a

Catholic priest means by the word pride. For him, pride is self-assertion against the duty of man to believe in and worship God. It is, therefore, the most pernicious and dangerous of sins.

The problem is that sin is a concept that doesn't resonate with me, so the argument has no effect. But I still strongly dislike being told that there is something fundamentally wrong with my life. I feel my face redden with a flush of anger. I reach for the door handle of the truck and put one foot on the running board.

"So what's so wrong with pride? In any event, it's the way I choose to live my life."

I climb into the truck and drive off, leaving the priest standing in the parking lot. I realize I've been pretty rude to the guy. I rationalize the rudeness with the argument that he started the fight. Besides, he's not likely to complain to my (Mormon) boss.

As I pull away, I realize that this may be the first time I have taken a stance with somebody other than my friends about being an atheist. I sense that I have just done one of those 'coming of age' things. I have out-grown the God of my childhood and early teenage years and now publicly nailed my colors to the mast of atheism.

Driving down the road in my bright red truck and pinstripes, I'm struck by the irony of what just happened. I have just made my atheist 'first confession' to a Catholic priest, of all people, and the first one I have ever met at that.

I take a deep breath and exhale slowly.

I expect this sort of proselytizing from the Mormons. After all, I grew up with them. But now I've been ambushed by a Catholic priest. In Mormon Territory, yet.

At the same time, I realize what made me angry about the priest's rebuke. The last two years have been tough, and I feel like I'm on the road to recovery. I wouldn't have gotten here without determination and self-respect – pride, if you will.

Yeah, my pride and arrogance got me into trouble. But that was then, and this is now. Pride is what gets you up off the mat when life – or your own stupidity – knocks you down. I tried the meek-as-a-mouse stuff and found that it doesn't work. And I'm not going back there.

When I moved here two years ago, Salt Lake City seemed like a big city compared to the small town in Idaho where I grew up. But now it's beginning to feel like an ill-fitting suit. It's still a very religious place. And I want a bigger, more intellectual, more broad-minded environment.

I think it's time to get out of Dodge.

CHAPTER 2
Wanderlust Sets In

Mid-March, Salt Lake City

I WASN'T PREPARED FOR LYDIA'S question.

"So, why Paris?"

Until we got into this conversation, I had never thought about studying in Europe. Now, I'm being challenged to defend why I would like to do it in Paris. I scramble for an answer.

"Paris seems logical to me. As you know, I'm a big fan of the French existentialist philosophers like Camus and Sartre and have a couple of years of French under my belt. I'm thinking it would be good to become fluent in French and get a better understanding of contemporary French literature as well as philosophy."

Lydia laughs and looks at me with an element of disbelief in her expression. "You're way too serious, David. The kids I know who went to Paris didn't have nearly as much fun as those who went to Vienna. I think the Austrians are much friendlier, and it's a much bigger program than Paris. "

"I didn't realize that fun was supposed to be the decisive criterion," I say sarcastically, at the same time letting a smile creep over my face to make sure Lydia knows I'm kidding – sort of.

Lydia and I are in this particular conversation somewhat by accident. Lydia is my new sister-in-law. She and Carl were married over Christmas, and in January Lydia moved from San Francisco to Utah, where Carl and I are both working on liberal arts degrees and trying to cope with the peculiar culture of Salt Lake City.

Lydia and I are close in age and we enjoy many of the same things, such as discussing literature and philosophy. Lydia is an only child, and I grew up in an all-male household, so we are both making the most of the brother-sister thing.

While I was waiting for her to turn up for our coffee date, I spotted an ad for the *Institute for European Studies* in the Utah Daily Chronicle. A little way into the conversation, I push the Daily Chronicle across the table.

"I'm toying with the idea of studying in Europe."

Lydia glances at the ad and gives me her best Cheshire Cat smile. "Wonderful. I have a number of friends who went on IES programs. My best friend from high school went to Vienna for a year and loved it."

Ah, yes. Why am I not surprised? I've never met anyone who studied in Europe and never traveled further east than Ohio. But Lydia's background is another story altogether. She grew up in Pennsylvania, the daughter of a stockbroker who likes to fish every summer in Sun Valley, which is where she and Carl met. Strikingly beautiful, she was an art history major at Mills College and has a lot more experience of the world than I do.

I'm slightly better prepared for her next question.

"So how will you pay for it?" Lydia knows that I'm working my way through college on part-time and summer jobs.

"Strangely enough, I think I might just be able to cover it between what I have in savings plus a hard push this summer."

Lydia laughs. "You're amazing. I can't believe you're working your way through college and saving money at the same time."

"Not amazing. Just determined to make up for past failings."

"In that case, I think the real question is what you want to get out of a year in Europe."

"Well, yeah, I suppose it is. My top of the head answer is change and adventure. As you know, I'm a little bored with Utah. Besides, ski season is nearly over..."

Lydia smiles at my reference to skiing. She's not a skier, but skiing is one of the things I like about Salt Lake City. The Utah campus is in the foothills of the Salt Lake Valley and a half an hour from some of the greatest powder skiing in the world. For the winter term, I arranged my classes to finish by mid-day, just in case there is fresh powder on afternoons when I'm not working.

Lydia then gets a serious look on her face.

"I think it would be great for you to get out of Utah and Idaho. I don't think you really fit into this culture. Europe would really expand your horizons. You could do so much more than just sit here in Salt Lake City."

"Are you suggesting that an atheist philosophy major might be just a tad uncomfortable in the heart of Mormonville?"

Lydia laughs.

"Is that why you're an atheist? Because you're surrounded by Mormons?"

I feel myself bristling at the suggestion that my atheism is a reaction to anything, much less the Mormons. I know Lydia is asking a simple question, not challenging my intellectual position, but she's touched a nerve.

"I'm an atheist because it's the only intellectually sound position out there. In any event, it's a far more rational than what is on offer from religion, including Mormonism, Catholicism and whatever other 'ism' you'd care to name."

Lydia laughs. "So tell me how you really feel, David."

I laugh too, but feel a need to change the topic and tone of the conversation.

"Back to your earlier question, I've had some great professors at Utah, but the ones I really connect with are the Europeans. I like the way they think and the breadth of their education, intellectual depth and willingness to challenge everything. For me, it would be a dream to be in a European university setting for as long as possible.

"Europe is also where much of the most interesting philosophy is being done. That's really the reason I thought about Paris first, because of my work on French existentialism and my admiration for Camus and Sartre. Vienna, on the other hand, could be a great spot to focus on logical positivism and Wittgenstein, not to mention Freud and some of the German schools of philosophy. So both are possibilities.

"In any event, I expect that a year in Europe would add something to my college resume and might help me get into a better grad school. It might even help me recover from my little high school disaster."

Lydia perks up. "What disaster was that?"

Oops. I really don't want to discuss this, but can't simply brush Lydia off.

"Something that was fun at the time, but turned out to be a colossally stupid maneuver on my part. I got kicked out of high school in the middle of my senior year."

Lydia leans forward and smiles in a conspiratorial way. "Gee, I like colossally stupid maneuvers. Tell me more."

"Hmm. I guess it started out as an intellectual challenge. I was student body president, and one of my tasks was to arrange for the printing of a student directory. I mentioned this to a couple of friends, and somehow it morphed into the idea of doing it ourselves. We knew little or nothing about printing, but that's what made it fun. We figured out what was required. Somehow, we came up with the idea of using the school district's print shop."

"Sounds reasonable. So what went wrong?"

"We didn't bother asking the school district for permission."

"You didn't? So how did you expect to get access to it?"

"One of my friends had access to a master key to the school system as part of his audio-visual work in the school auditorium. So we figured we could print the directory at night over a weekend. The clandestine nature of the exercise simply made the intellectual challenge all the more exciting."

"Did you do it?"

"Oh, yeah. We worked our butts off typing 1600 names and addresses onto offset stencils – meticulously correcting and proofreading every entry. We then bought all the materials and produced a couple of thousand folded, bound and stapled copies with a custom artwork cover over a weekend. We delivered the directories on Monday morning, claiming that a professional printer had done the job. Most people thought it was really good work.

"So what happened?"

"We left some trash in the print shop, which eventually led to our getting caught."

Lydia laughs. "What an insane thing to do!"

I take a sip of cold coffee. "What was insane? The whole idea? Or leaving misprinted pages in the print shop trash can?"

"I guess the whole project is amazing. The fact that you figured out how to do it, spent your evenings and weekends typing and printing, and then delivered a professional product without any prior experience."

"Yeah, we were pretty proud of what we had done – apart from the fact that we earned about 10 cents an hour doing it. Unfortunately, the school administrators were not impressed. But I think they were a tiny bit embarrassed by the fact that students had been given access to a system-wide master key. Technically, we could claim we weren't breaking and entering, but it was hard to argue that we weren't using school property without permission.

"In the end, the administration opted to boot us out of school for a few days and remove us from student activities. Which in my case brought an end to my career as student body president."

"Worse things could happen. Why do you think it was such a disaster?"

I stare at the coffee residue in the bottom of my cup for a moment.

"It was a very public humiliation. I had had a very successful career in student politics, I was near the top of my class academically, with good SATs, and I had excellent college prospects. Unfortunately, on the basis of some less than terrific advice, I had applied to only one college – Reed. After the printing press disaster, one of my teachers decided that I wasn't 'sufficiently penitent', and she withdrew her college recommendation. As a result, Reed still accepted me but pulled the plug on any prospect of a scholarship.

"So instead of heading off to an elite school on somebody else's nickel, I had to find a place that I could afford on the basis of summer and part-time employment. Utah became the default option. To top it off, my girl friend dumped me."

"Ouch! It sounds like a terrible experience." Lydia looks at me with a curious mixture of disbelief and compassion. I'm not sure if the 'ouch' refers to losing a scholarship or a girl friend or both.

"It was a tough six months of being angry, rejected and depressed. But it's what got me interested in moral philosophy."

"Really? Tell me how."

"It was the ethical lapse involved. I did something I knew was wrong, but rationalized it as a kind of elaborate teenage prank. And we were too cocky to think that we could get caught.

"At first, the big question was, 'how could I be so stupid?' But then I realized the problem was deeper: what is it that causes ethical failure and moral blindness like this? How does a guy with a good background and lots to lose throw it all away for the thrill of doing something clever and risky?"

Lydia moves her empty coffee cup aside and leans across the table. "I think the Greeks called it *hubris*."

I think for a minute. "You mean, like the hero who presses ahead in search of the truth despite being warned that he won't like what he finds?"

"Just a bit." Lydia smiles. "Anyway, I think you should go to Vienna. You'll need a second foreign language for grad school and you'll get an entirely different perspective on Europe than you would in Paris."

Lydia heads off to her next class, and I sit for a while thinking about my somewhat prickly response to Lydia's comment about why I'm an atheist.

CHAPTER 3

The Fraud God

Mid-March, Salt Lake City

DESPITE MY PHILOSOPHICAL STANCE WITH Lydia, the truth is that I didn't become an atheist purely through logical argument. Like nearly everyone in small town America, I grew up with religion, albeit somewhat unconventionally. Eastern Idaho is – even more than Salt Lake City – predominantly Mormon, which put my family in a minority. We were Christian Scientists.

My childhood God is best described as The Comfort God.

I remember an incident after mother died. I was probably in the 4th grade, sad, withdrawn and feeling very much alone, probably suffering from undiagnosed (and untreated) depression. I have a vivid memory of standing on the playground watching the other fourth grade boys playing baseball at recess. Out of nowhere the thought occurred to me that mother had been a very beautiful woman, and God had taken her to heaven to be with him. Almost immediately, the sadness lifted, and I ran off to join the recess baseball game.

The Comfort God was a lot of help during those childhood years.

This was also a time when I experienced the best side of Mormonism. The Ladies Aid Society showed up the day after mother died with food and offers of help without regard to the fact that we were not Mormons. Later, the Mormon high school choir director scooped up a lonely 10-year old and took him along to choir practice, where the high school kids treated me like a younger brother. I also got included in Mormon Cub Scouts, Mormon softball, Mormon after school activities, and Mormon anything else I cared to join.

My Christian Science beliefs weren't a terrific amount of help. As they say, it's neither Christian nor science. But the practice of Christian Science involves a discipline of Bible reading along with Mary Baker Eddy's metaphysical view of disease and the world generally. Besides acquiring a precocious vocabulary, I also memorized Jesus' Beatitudes, the second of which goes something like, 'blessed are those who mourn, for they shall be comforted.'

Some people 'lose their faith' – or at least have it severely tested – by the death of a parent or some similar event. They start out asking, 'how could God allow this to happen?' They end up rejecting the whole idea of God. I didn't have this problem. When I was about three years old, my mother suffered what was politely called 'a nervous breakdown' and was in and out of mental hospitals until she died when I was about ten. There were good moments when she was home. And there were bad ones such as the unpredictable rages at dinnertime when she started throwing the dishes at the walls.

My best memories of her are from the time she took me with her to live with her mother in Boise. Life was orderly and peaceable, and I had mother, grandmother and Aunt Olive to myself. Unfortunately, that period was pretty tough for my father and Carl.

I don't remember ever blaming God for what happened to mother. She was sick, and she died young. It was just one of those things that happens in life. Sometimes mothers die young. Her death probably left me with emotional scars, but nothing more crippling than trouble sustaining long-term relationships with girlfriends.

Then there was the morning just before the end of my first grade year when I jumped out of bed and couldn't walk. Polio fear bounced around the house for a couple of days until the diagnosis came back as rheumatic fever. I spent the summer in bed, and I remember my Dad reading Psalms to me at night. It was part of his Swedish Lutheran background, and part of our Christian Science practice.

I guess that's why I felt that The Comfort God was real. I needed a lot of comfort, and he showed up at critical times – even if it was all taking place in my head.

The same was not true of my teenage God.

I maintained the Christian Science study program well into Jr. High. I remember a positive effect from mornings when I read the Bible and Mrs. Eddy. But then a real 'crisis of faith' developed. For reasons that were a mystery to me at the time, a set of faster-developer classmates decided I was the perfect target for harassment and bullying.

I went through what seemed like a very long period of trying to avoid threatened or actual efforts to beat me up. I got serious about prayer (as understood by a 13 year old Christian Scientist) – in particular, prayers for 'deliverance from my enemies'. I prayed and dodged and prayed and dodged. I 'turned the other cheek' thinking that would help induce God to deliver me sooner and more effectively.

But no help came.

One day during lunch hour, in the main hall of the school, one of my regular tormentors hit me in the shoulder and I hit him back. This caught him by surprise for a moment, but then he came after me. I had made up my mind not to back down, and I went after him with everything I had. We slugged our way up and down the hall with books and other students scattering in all directions. It's what you do in an Idaho farming town.

The fight didn't last long. We both realized about the same time that we were about 50 feet from the Principal's office. He offered to call it quits, and I agreed.

That was the end of the bullying. My life got better, and my theology began to evolve.

The first big, deep insight was that 'God helps those who help themselves'. The second was that Jesus' Sermon on the Mount was for weaklings and fools. And, no, the meek are not going to inherit the earth. Finally, the conviction gradually emerged that the teenage God of Deliverance was a fraud. He didn't show up when I needed him.

I started to formulate a personal philosophy of self-reliance and self-determination. My attitude toward authority and behavioral norms began to look very much like, well, a teenager. I didn't want to be told what I couldn't do. And I didn't want a lot of moral advice from others, particularly since 'morality' in my small Mormon town was pretty much synonymous with 'sex'. On top of that, I could rationalize my rebellion pretty well as a rejection of the heavily religious and – to my mind – hypocritical culture around me.

By the time I hit high school, I was well on my way to becoming a formal atheist and cynic. It was clear to me that God was unreliable, inept, out of touch and irrelevant.

And nonexistent.

In the end, the Mormon culture around me had little to do with my becoming an atheist. But it had a lot to do with the decision to study philosophy.

It was pretty obvious in small town eastern Idaho that religious belief and practice provided the dominant framework of social rules and expectations. But *if* there is no God, then the whole social apparatus is based on ignorance, lies and/or self-deception. When I came to realize that God *doesn't in fact exist*, I saw a need for a new foundation for society based on reason rather than religion – which was doomed to lose its moral purchase on society as educational levels increased and religious adherence declined.

So philosophy became a kind of calling for me, aimed not so much at disproving the existence of God as formulating what should take the place of religion in society. This wasn't something I thought should be left to chance. And it was a cause to which I thought I could contribute in a significant way. My low opinion of the Mormons was thus not because I thought their particular beliefs are inferior to other religions, but simply because they happened to be the dominant culture around me.

In thinking further about the conversation with Lydia, I realize that going to Europe is as much a way of breaking free of the past as it is about a new adventure. Despite being a thoroughgoing atheist, I still feel the constraint of this peculiar Mormon culture of Eastern Idaho and Salt Lake City.

My head is somewhere else. I want my experience to be somewhere else as well, in a culture that is intellectual, secular and 'beyond religion.'

CHAPTER 4

Dreaming Among the Spires

Early September, Oxford

"YOU KNOW, ANYONE CAN HAVE an English-style lawn."

Danny and I were walking through the main quad of Christ Church College on a guided tour with a group of American college students. This is the first day of the three-week tour of Europe that is part of the Vienna program laid on by the Institute for European Studies – or IES for short. We arrived in Oxford late last night by bus from Southampton.

Danny and I met on the boat from New York and became immediate friends. Danny is a student at a Pennsylvania liberal arts college, reading a lot of the same books and subjects as I am. He's also charming, a smooth operator with the opposite sex, and a very humorous cynic.

Danny and I also share the experience of being minorities in cultures dominated by religion. Having grown up Jewish in Philadelphia, Danny has a lot of practical experience with Catholics, much of it connected to ethnic competition with the Irish and the Italians.

In my case, it's the Mormons. As one of my father's Jewish friends likes to say, 'Eastern Idaho is the only place in the world where a Catholic is a Protestant and a Jew is a Gentile'.

I look at Danny, knowing that there is a punch line on its way. I decide to play the straight man. "Oh yeah. And how is that?"

"It's really quite simple: you plant the grass where it can get rained on every day, mow it often, and roll it whenever it needs it. Just keep that up for 400 years, and you'll have a lawn like that one over there." Danny smiles.

"Hmm. I guess I better send a telegram to my dad to tell him to get started right away."

We both laugh and suddenly realize that the group of students has stopped in front of us and the tour guide is waiting for us to pay attention.

She begins. "Oxford University is the second oldest university in the world and the oldest English speaking university. Teaching began in Oxford in the 11th century, and the university was formally founded in 1167 following the expulsion of foreign students from Paris. At first, the students were dispersed in private residences, but as conflict began to develop between the students and the general population – so-called 'town and gown' conflicts – special purpose residence halls were built that evolved into walled colleges such as Christ Church."

She goes on to describe the history of Christ Church, Tom Tower, the Cathedral in its midst, its art gallery and its dining hall, all of which we walk through on the tour.

All of which adds to my sense of sensory overload. Oxford is absolutely spectacular. Our 'digs', as the English say, are in St. Hilda's College, one of the four women's colleges in Oxford. St. Hilda's dates from the late 19th century, and the college is built in a late Victorian gothic revival style. Accommodation is correspondingly Spartan. No reason to pamper the girls, I guess.

We started our walking tour by crossing Magdalen Bridge, cut through an amazing Rose Garden and then walked along the back wall of Merton College. The view over the rugby and cricket fields to Christ Church Meadow seems quintessentially English. The fact that the colleges are interwoven with the town gives the University a very different feel from the typical purpose built university campus in the States. I love it.

There's also something incredibly serene about the place. Not everywhere, of course. The High Street is choked with traffic, even though the students have yet to 'come up' for the fall term. Red double-decker buses maneuver around corners and up the streets at what seems to be reckless speed – on the wrong side of the road! But on the Meadow and here inside Christ Church College, it's quiet, unhurried, and imposing.

We walk out the back gate of Christ Church, past Corpus Christi, and take a short tour of Merton with its beautiful views over the Meadow and then come back around the front of Oriel to the High Street, aiming for Radcliffe Square. As we walk down the High, the guide points out the façade of the Rhodes Building that is part of Oriel College, with its statue of one of Oriel's most famous students, Cecil Rhodes.

We stop in front of the Radcliffe Camera, an 18th century round library, which stands in the center of the square, surrounded by All Souls College, Brasenose College, St. Mary the Virgin Church and the Bodleian Library. My mind drifts back to Oriel and Cecil Rhodes.

One of my finest high school experiences was a senior world history course, taught by a demanding teacher – Miss Neuber – who discussed Rhodes and the Rhodes Scholarships with awe as part of our study of European imperialism. I got the impression that she regarded Rhodes Scholars as the pinnacle of academic achievement, and I made a mental note to look into the Rhodes for grad school. Neuber was also the one who steered me towards Reed College – the 'Harvard of the West' – though not the one who gave me the advice to apply to Reed only.

My relationship with Neuber actually began in my junior year, when I was allowed to sit her American history exam and ended up besting her elite junior history students as well as all of her senior world history classes. Our relationship ended when she withdrew her college recommendation after my fall from grace in my senior year, but by that time she had fired my interest in history and given me facts and information that are coming to life in new ways as I proceed into my year in Vienna. And now her lecture on Rhodes and the Rhodes Scholars is rekindling a desire to do significant things in life as I walk among the colleges of Oxford.

I tune back into the guide. "Most of the buildings in Oxford are individual colleges. On your left, for example, you can see the library of All Souls College."

Everyone rotates 90 degrees left. Amazingly, as if on cue, the sun breaks through the clouds and lights up the sandstone buildings and 'dreaming spires' of All Souls. It's incredibly beautiful despite the century of grime and soot sticking to the college wall and some of the buildings.

"The Bodleian Library is to the north behind you, and incorporates the Divinity School, which is perhaps the most beautiful medieval building in Oxford. The Divinity School is the oldest surviving building that was built by the University itself rather than one of the colleges."

Everyone turns again to see where the guide is pointing, which requires either a further 90 degree left turn, or if you happen to turn back to the guide first, a full 270 turn to the right.

The guide then strides off in the direction of the Bodleian Library, and we all dutifully fall in line behind her. We proceed through the gate, cross the quad with its multiple staircases labeled 'School of Logic', School of Metaphysics', etc. and enter a very gothic hall.

"The Divinity School was built in the last half of the 15th century to provide a setting for the theology faculty's lectures and debates. The hall we are in is the Convocation House. It was built in the early 17th century and is still used for University functions."

One of the students asks, "Is Oxford still a religious school?"

'Dumb question', I think. The guide smiles.

"The University was never a religious school in the sense of being sponsored or controlled by the church. Until the 11th century, most higher education was provided by Cathedral schools and monasteries, mainly for the purpose of educating the clergy. Oxford, like other medieval universities, developed in the context of increased urbanization and rising incomes and wealth, as well as recognition that higher education was an asset to the Crown and the nobility.

"The University was nonetheless deeply Christian in outlook and curriculum. Theology was held in high regard not just because of the role of the church but also because it was seen as the foundation for other knowledge. Since God made the world, one needed to understand God in order to understand the world.

"The University crest, which you can see on the wall behind you, shows the University's motto."

Another 180-degree rotation.

"'*Dominus illuminatio mea*' is Latin for 'The Lord is my light'. It reflects a medieval belief that human beings achieve insight and understanding –

'illumination' in medieval terms – as a consequence of being made in the image of God."

'Dominus illuminatio mea', I say to myself a couple of times, to get the cadence right. The roots of religion obviously run very deep in European culture. No wonder it's proven so hard to eradicate.

We move on down the High to Magdalen College, the last stop on our tour and just across the Cherwell River from St. Hilda's. In quirky English fashion, Magdalen is pronounced more like 'mawd-lyn' than the way it is spelled. Mercifully, the guide is focused on only two aspects of Magdalen – the deer park and the Cloister. This afternoon's schedule includes a couple of lectures on English history and politics.

We come to a halt in the Cloister. "Magdalen College was founded in the 15th century and is one of the larger colleges in the University. C.S. Lewis was a long-time fellow of Magdalen College. The Cloister is another outstanding example of gothic architecture in Oxford."

There is something welcoming about the Cloister. It encloses another of those 400-year-old English lawns, visible through the delicate gothic columns on all sides. It's easy to imagine dons and students walking around the Cloister debating some obscure topic like how many angels can dance on the head of a pin. No urgency, no need for the debate to be about something commercial or even practical, just a pursuit of knowledge and truth for its own sake.

'Now this,' I say to myself, 'would be a great place to go to school.'

CHAPTER 5

Censers and Pythons

Mid September, Maria Laach Abbey

WE'RE ABOUT TWO WEEKS INTO the tour now. Besides Oxford, we've been to London, Canterbury, Bruges, Brussels, Paris, Chartres, Rheims, Trier, Cologne, various other places along the way, and now the Rhine Valley – including a boat ride up the Rhine past the Lorelei Rock and the now defunct castles of the original robber barons.

Given the prominence of Christianity in European culture and history, it seems like every stop involves a tour of a church or cathedral, and today is no exception. This afternoon's agenda includes a visit to an 11th century Benedictine monastery called Maria Laach.

It's a spectacular day – sunny and warm – and the German countryside is incredibly beautiful. The leaves are starting to turn and the grape harvest is underway.

Maria Laach is on the tour because it is considered a (restored) masterpiece of German Romanesque architecture. It's also a major tourist attraction. The parking lot is full of cars and tour buses, and multiple tour groups are making their way through the abbey.

Our tour was timed for the late afternoon so that the Catholic students in the program could stay for Vespers. As the tour finishes, I head for the exit. Just before I get to the door, I run into Frau Doctor Benesch. The Frau Doctor is the Austrian art history professor who has been steering us from one place to the other over the past two weeks. Single, late thirties, with bright, clear blue eyes that shine when she's talking about art history and hold your gaze when she's in one on one conversation.

"David, aren't you going to stay for the service?" she asks.

By this stage, Benesch knows most of the students, especially the ones like me who ask a lot of questions. Something tells me Benesch is not asking an idle question.

"No, not really," I reply with as much nonchalance as I can muster. "I'm not Catholic so this really isn't my thing."

This is the half-truth that I hope will get me out the door in as little time as possible. In fact, the church tours and history are beginning to wear on my atheist sensitivities. I can cope as long as it stays on the level of art or cultural history, but I'm strongly resistant to religious ceremonies. I've taken to offsetting my frustrations by tweaking some of the more religious students with cynical comments about religion generally. At times I can be aggressive about my atheism, and in any event, I'm perfectly willing to take on someone who wants to argue about religion or, worse, try to convert me, as I half suspect Benesch is about to do.

The Frau Doctor takes a different approach.

"I was thinking that you might enjoy seeing an example of 11th century liturgy. The buildings of the monastery have been restored but so has the liturgy. I think you might find it interesting," she says with a smile and that penetrating, blue-eyed gaze.

Behind her, the heavy wooden doors of the western portal are open, and the afternoon sun is spreading over the abbey's well-worn stone flooring.

I hesitate. I look at the doors, then back at Benesch. She's standing next to one of the thousand-year-old pillars at the back of the sanctuary. I could be out of here in about four strides. But I make a fateful choice.

"OK, I'll stay for a few minutes just to see a bit of the liturgy."

"Good," she says, "I think you'll really enjoy it." Another warm smile.

I position myself facing the altar with my back to the pillar, and in easy access to the door. I plan to leave as soon as Benesch goes forward to find a seat. Unfortunately, she just stays where she is, next to the pillar. And right next to me. The doors close, and my eyes struggle to adjust to the abrupt loss of bright sunlight

The abbey is laid out in the traditional Latin cross. The simple Romanesque arches and pillars are refreshing after the ornate design and décor of the gothic cathedrals that have been our diet for the last two weeks. The stained glass windows transform the afternoon sun into a rose colored light. Someone lights candles on the altar. The pews are full.

The service begins, and the monks enter through a door on the right side of the chapel and begin singing as they proceed across the chapel and turn up the center aisle towards the altar. A monk at the front swings a censer. The rest hold their hands in front of them in an attitude of prayer. The monks are dressed in dark brown robes with hoods pulled back. They walk slowly, in rhythm to the Latin chant. They're not in any hurry, but there's a purposive quality to their procession. The smell of the incense begins to fill the church, and the smoke rises in the rose colored light.

The monks proceed up the aisle to the choir stalls, take their seats and move through the vespers liturgy. The Gregorian chant reverberates in the Abbey. I am dimly aware of people in the congregation sitting, kneeling, crossing themselves – things I don't really understand but just accept as part of a ritual that is about as distant from my experience as Mars. It occurs to me that this is the first time I have been in a religious service in a Catholic church.

At the same time, I find the whole thing riveting. I watch the monks' every move, particularly the guy with the censer. I try to catch Latin words that I recognize, I listen for the rise and fall of the melody, the complex, shifting harmonies of all male voices, the interplay of the slowing fading rose colored light and the smell of the incense. It's an assault on the senses, and there is something subtly mysterious and otherworldly about it.

Then – abruptly it seems to me – the monks get up to leave. Singing a last chant, they file back down the aisle, turn, and exit the sanctuary in the same way they came in. The door to the chapter house closes behind them, leaving the smell and smoke of the incense silently lingering in the air. The service is over, and after a long pause people start to get up from where they have been kneeling or sitting in the pews.

I stand for a moment in the back of the chapel, staring at the door to the chapter house. I blink a couple of times, as though awakening from a trance, and the first thing I'm aware of is that I haven't shifted weight on my feet since the service started. How and why I know this I'm not sure. But it's the first indication of how totally focused I have been, almost transfixed by the vespers service. I've been rooted to the floor next to the pillar.

Then another strange feeling overtakes me. I feel powerfully drawn towards the door where the monks entered and exited. I'm not ready for the service to be over. And I want to go where these guys have gone. Something in this abbey, in this service, is pulling at me, stirring a longing that is both mysterious and too deep for words.

I shake my head in an attempt to clear the confusion. What is this feeling, this longing, and where has it come from? The Frau Doctor is still there next to me.

"Well, what did you think?"

The main doors open again. I'm somewhere between speechless and incoherent. "Interesting," I mumble, trying to avoid eye contact and any further conversation with Benesch.

I turn and join the congregation in a slow shuffle out the doors, staring somewhat blankly at the setting sun. As I walk out of the Abbey, I realize that something fundamentally odd or mysterious just happened. While I can think of a number of common sense reasons for my feelings, none quite seem to capture the mystery.

After all, I'm an atheist. There is no God. Therefore, this longing, this deep, almost cosmic, longing cannot be for Him, no matter how many people interpret such experiences that way. It must be something else, an unusual aesthetic reaction to music, sound, light, and setting.

But then...maybe...what if...?

I begin to feel a bit like the guy in the jungle adventure movie who is attacked by a giant python. The python has wrapped itself around my body and is threatening to squeeze the life out of me. 'If I can just get my free hand on my knife, I can stab this thing and make it let go...'

Fortunately, a metaphorical knife is within reach.

I start to tell myself, 'this can't be happening, this can't be happening.' Stab. Stab. 'There is a perfectly natural explanation for these feelings. This isn't some God thing, just an aesthetic experience.' Stab again.

I begin to calm down. The python loosens its grip a bit.

'Maybe the guy with the censer is a sorcerer, or there's some other similarly smart, highly intellectual explanation for it.' The python starts to uncoil. I take a deep breath and slowly exhale.

But then the python tightens again. If this had been just an aesthetic experience, the logical reaction would have been to want the monks to stay longer or come back. *But I wanted to go with them.* Why the sensation of being drawn, called into their world? Why this unexpected and mysterious *longing?*

I shake my head again, still trying to clear my thoughts. 'These things happen,' I tell myself, 'after being in too many churches too many days in a row. Pull yourself together.' Another stab.

The python lets go and begins to slither off into the setting sun. But I can still feel its coils around my neck, and the nagging question, 'what the hell was going on in there?'

I look out across the German countryside and imagine centuries of people working the fields around the Abbey and attending Sunday vespers. I begin to relax again, and a peaceful feeling settles on me. It's a very beautiful evening in a very beautiful place.

Maybe this is all that happened in the Abbey. No great mystery, just an unusual aesthetic experience. Maybe it's just a good reminder of the dangers of religion and the way emotions can sometimes overwhelm reason. Best to chalk the experience to being caught off guard. 'The Mystery of Maria Laach' is no different than the peaceful feeling of watching a German sunset. It will soon fade away and be replaced by a new day.

Or so I expect.

CHAPTER 6

Death of a Jaeger

All Saints Weekend, Mariazell

ON HALLOWEEN I HITCHHIKED WITH a friend from Vienna to Marizell. Actually, it wasn't Halloween in Austria, but All Souls Day, which is linked with All Saints Day (November 1) into a long weekend, one of the few advantages that I can see to having a state sanctioned church.

Mark and I went to Mariazell at the Frau Doctor's suggestion because it is the most important pilgrimage site in Austria and therefore of significant cultural and historical interest. And on All Souls Day, it is packed with Austrians and other nationalities making pilgrimages or just having fun on a delightful fall weekend.

We did the obligatory tour of the Baroque cathedral with its supposedly miracle-working image of the Virgin Mary dating from the 12th century. The interior of the church is overwhelming. There are candles everywhere, along with altars, crosses and people going through the motions of religion.

Despite all the candlepower, the interior is still dark. I wonder how they keep from burning the place down on a regular basis. I learn that the Turks did it for them on several occasions, along with various other invaders and reformers, and I again get a sense of the durability of religious belief and practice in European history.

Returning to the afternoon sunshine brought a sense of relief. Mark, who is Catholic, got more out of the visit than I did, and we browse through the stores so he can pick up some souvenirs to send back to the US.

This part of Austria is incredibly beautiful. Mariazell is a very pretty town with narrow streets, painted stucco buildings, tile roofs, window boxes full of flowers and lots of people wearing traditional Austrian dress – *Dirndls* for the girls, grayish Loden jackets and short pants/long socks for the guys.

Given our lack of forward planning, Mark and I end up spending the night in a *Gasthaus* in a neighboring village. This entails a long walk in the dark, since the buses are infrequent and there is very little car traffic and a natural reluctance to pick up a couple of foreigners in the dark. And dark it is. Clouds block out any star or moonlight, and the farmhouses are small and set well back from the road. We stick to the pavement as best as possible, essentially feeling our way down a single lane road.

The lights of the *Gasthaus* act like a beacon over the last few hundred yards of our trip through the Austrian night. A friendly blond in a *Dirndl* checks us in and gives us our room key. We lug our backpacks up the stairs to a simply furnished, well aired (i.e., cold) bedroom with clean linens and large down comforters. There's a sink with a mirror in the corner, with a WC and bathtub somewhere down the hall.

As we go down to dinner, a band starts playing in the *Stube*. It's a traditional Austrian village band with tuba, trumpet, accordion, drums and a few other instruments. The *Stube*, which doubles as dining room, bar, village hall and social gathering spot is filling up with locals and a few tourists. Mark and I are clearly the only Americans.

We sit down at one of the shared tables, exchange '*Grüss Gotts*' with an older couple sitting at the other end of the table and order dinner. The beer is excellent and the sausage and kraut perfect. The evening has a distinctly festive air. Many of the patrons sing along with the band – another endearing Austrian custom.

As we eat and listen to the music, I notice a group of older men seated together and dressed in what look like green Loden uniforms – short jackets, knee length pants, long socks and peaked Loden caps with elk hair brushes stuck in the hat band. They appear to be in their 50s and 60s with a few distinctly older, tapping along to the music, sometimes singing, sometimes just listening quietly. Their conversation is sparse and quiet with an occasional smile or short laugh at some funny story.

One man in particular fascinates me. I guess he must be in his 70s. His face is weathered, his hair and mustache white. The lines run deep around the eyes, like a man who has squinted into the summer sun and coped with the glare on winter snow for decade after decade. The look on his face is serene, peaceable, like someone who has lived well and whose concerns are few and focused on today.

As I'm studying the Ancient Austrian, the woman sharing our table slides down the bench and asks me in perfect English if Mark and I are students. She introduces herself and her husband as teachers from Vienna who have come to Mariazell for the weekend – Herr Doctor and Frau Wilhelm.

The four of us chat in English about life in Austria vs. the US, what we're studying, why we chose Austria, what we think, etc. When the conversation lags, I nod in the direction of the old men in green, and ask Frau Wilhem about them.

"They're *Jaeger*. I noticed that you were watching them."

"I'm sorry, *Jaeger?*"

"They're the local *Jaeger*, or hunters. It's an honored position in a village like this. They function as game wardens and also hunt to control the population of wild animals in the area. Occasionally, they have to deal with dangerous animals that might threaten livestock or people."

Game wardens. So that explains the uniform.

"Interesting. So what's going on this evening? Is this a kind of special event where they're being honored?"

"No," says Frau Wilhelm, "today they buried one of their friends, a fellow *Jaeger*, and they have come here to celebrate. It's probably someone they grew up with and have known all their lives."

I'm a bit stunned by the natural way Frau Wilhelm says this, as though she were telling me what she had for dinner.

"Celebrate?" I ask with obvious astonishment. "Why would they be celebrating the death of a close friend?"

"Because he was a friend and he was an important part of their lives. They believe that he has gone to a better place. Their way of honoring him is to celebrate his life. The funeral was earlier today. We happened to see the procession from the church to the graveyard with all of the *Jaeger* following the coffin."

I look at Frau Wilhelm, then back at the Ancient Austrian. He's tapping his foot to the rhythm of the music, a distant look in his eyes, but still that same serene expression.

For a moment, I feel like I've been transported to a parallel universe. I'm talking to an intelligent, well-educated woman who talks about death in a matter of fact way and watching a man who just lost one of his best friends but looks like he has just gone down to the local bar for a Saturday night drink. This doesn't remotely resemble the American way of death that I know.

Frau Wilhelm sips her beer, listens to the music and waits for me to absorb the scene.

After a long pause, she says, "It's the way their faith works. Their belief in God bridges both life and death. A long life is a great blessing, something to be thankful for. In Vienna, you find some people who have such a faith. But here in the mountains, close to nature, such a faith comes quite naturally."

"I see," I say, trying to process all of this in my atheist framework. Mark and the Wilhelms get into a conversation about their common Catholic background, and I tune out, still studying the men in green.

For me, death is the big issue to be resolved. It is the great enemy that swallows up life, love, and meaning. Death takes away everything we cherish and the fact that human beings can reflect on and anticipate their own death from an early age is a paradox.

Camus frames this paradox in terms of meaning: life is without meaning, yet we need meaning in order to live. Camus' heroes are people who nonetheless choose to live in the face of this 'absurdity'. I think I understand the argument, but I find it deeply unsatisfying.

Here in this Austrian *Gasthaus*, on All Saints weekend, I see in a new way that religion provides a way of integrating life and death, especially a religion like Christianity with its beliefs in heaven, resurrection, eventual justice and immortality of the soul. The Ancient Austrian and his friends have found peace and personal significance through their Catholicism – at least according to Frau Wilhem.

Unfortunately, it's just a set of beliefs, no more true that Santa Claus. To embrace such beliefs as a way of resolving the death issue strikes me as intellectually dishonest and cowardly, perhaps not for my *Jaeger* friend but certainly for me. To live and die in a small village in the Austrian mountains without ever facing a challenge to one's beliefs is one thing. But for someone who has 'seen the light', you can never go back, never 'go home again' to borrow Thomas Wolfe's phrase.

The Catholic culture runs deep in the Austrian mountains and valleys. Is it because the religion itself has been deeply inculcated in the people? Or because the people find it an easily accessible explanation of everything, one that enables them to deal with life and death?

In any event, it is a distant culture for me, not just because I grew up among the Mormons of Idaho, but because my atheism includes the rebuilding of culture around a more straightforward and intellectual set of propositions. I doubt that my Ancient Austrian friend would survive in the harsher climate of a sophisticated urban culture, where the examined life is a way of life.

No, there must be a better way of coming to terms with death. Stoicism in one of its variants. Acceptance of death as a fact. Finding a philosophy of life that remains reason-based in all respects yet enables one to live with the absurdity that we can anticipate death and its consequences without being driven to despair and desperation.

The band plays on, the oompahs dimly resonating in my ears.

Celebrate death? I hate death.

CHAPTER 7

Hitchhiking with the Holy Ghost

December, German-Austrian Border

HITCHHIKING IN EUROPE HAS A number of advantages.

It's free, culturally acceptable, offers a way to practice my German language skills, and an opportunity to meet a lot of people. And, it's usually somewhat of an adventure.

The adventure part has me stranded at the *Autobahn* crossing from Germany into Austria.

The purpose of the weekend trip to Munich in early December with a couple of friends was a combination of tourism and Christmas shopping for relatives back home. We had a good time but decided to split up on the way back to make the hitchhiking easier. Unfortunately, it's still taken most of Sunday and three different rides to get to the border. And now the challenge is to find someone who will carry me the rest of the way to Vienna.

Normally, the border is a great place to get a ride, if only because people have to stop and show their passports. This makes them more accessible to hitchhikers and less able to simply speed by with no eye contact.

However, being Sunday, most cars were full and drivers have an easy excuse to give a shrug and a gesture to the effect that 'they would love to give me a ride but unfortunately there just isn't room.'

I decided to hang around in the customs clearing area. It's cold, starting to get dark, raining slightly, and past my dinnertime. I put my thumb out, wave, smile, do everything I can think of to get drivers' attention.

I begin to think I might have to do something desperate (like take the train) when a guy gets out of his car to head into the customs office. He turns to someone in the car and says, in an American southern accent, "you stay here with the children, honey. I'll be right back."

I drift around the back of his car and note the W in the license plate number that indicates that he lives in Vienna. Bingo! This is an opportunity not to be missed.

I catch up to the guy on his way back to his car. He's in his thirties, medium build, brown hair, dressed in a kind of Texas meets Austria way.

"So how would you like to give an American student a ride back to Vienna?" I ask. I catch him by surprise.

He hesitates a moment, then says, "Sorry but our car is full," and walks off. Damn. Now I really am going to have to take the train.

Then he stops, slowly turns around, and walks back to me.

"Yes, I would like to give you a ride. It will be a bit crowded, but I think we can all fit in."

He opens the passenger door and asks his wife, "Honey, would you mind moving into the back seat with the kids. We're going to give this young man a ride back to Vienna."

She starts to protest, and I hear some grumbling from the back seat as the three tired kids realize they will be squeezed together with mom in the European version of a family sedan.

"I'm David", he says, reaching out to shake my hand, "and this is my wife Ellen."

"Hi," I reply, "my name is also David."

I shake his hand, a bit warily, as my gut tells me there's something more to David's decision to offer me a ride than just being nice. Ellen gets out of the car and shakes my hand, graciously. She's obviously tired, but nonetheless willing to help a stranger.

As we're squeezing my backpack into the trunk, David has to move a case of Dr. Pepper.

"The Dr. Pepper is a special treat," he says. "We have some friends in Munich who get it for us at the American army base."

I climb into the front seat, feeling just a tad guilty but very glad to be delivered from the cold and damp on the Austrian border.

We drive off and begin getting acquainted. Where are you from, what brings you here, etc. David and his wife are from Texas. He's a minister who leads a church in the suburbs of Vienna. I gather that he's an evangelist who is trying to convert the Austrian Catholics to some sort of American religious innovation.

I begin to sense where the conversation is going, but realize I'm stuck in this situation for a good three or four hours. While I now feel even more awkward, David and his family are being incredibly nice to me. I feign interest. At least, they aren't Mormons.

After some general background conversation, David gets out a Bible, opens it on the seat between us and proceeds to drive down the crowded *Autobahn*, through the rain and dark, with one hand on the wheel and one hand flipping pages in the Bible. I'm not terribly reassured and keep monitoring David's driving as we roll down the road.

"You see", he says pointing to a place in the Bible, "after Jesus was raised from the dead, he told his disciples to stay in Jerusalem until they were filled with the Holy Ghost and power. You can read it right here in the Bible."

David glances up to make a badly needed course correction. My attention shifts between where David's finger is pointing in the Bible and where we're headed on the *Autobahn*.

"Then, on the day of Pentecost, the Holy Ghost came on the disciples and they were all filled with power and began to speak in tongues."

I'm torn between being polite and desperately trying to figure out how to change the subject. Politeness wins by default, and I listen attentively while being *very* careful not to ask any questions.

He shows me other places in the Bible where it talks about the Holy Ghost, ending in a spot where someone says to someone else, 'did you receive the Holy Ghost when you believed?' and the response is, 'we didn't even know there was a Holy Ghost.'

I suddenly feel a kinship with the guys who didn't know there was a Holy Ghost.

David continues.

"In the early church, being baptized in the Holy Spirit was the norm, and Christianity spread across all countries and peoples. The early Christians had the power of the Spirit and were able to do miracles and other signs and wonders."

He looks up to see if I'm listening, glances at the road, and hearing no objection from me, rolls right along with his sermon. I just wish he would pay more attention to the 'signs' on the *Autobahn* and 'do the wonder' of focusing on his driving.

David then starts talking about how the Holy Spirit popped up again at the beginning of the 20th century.

"The Holy Spirit was poured out in four different places around the world, all independently of each other."

For some reason, I find this last point intriguing. David is obviously sincere and I have no reason to think he's making this up. The 19th century was full of religious innovations in America, notably Christian Science and Mormonism plus a slew of other cults and spinoffs. But something that was more global, in the 20th century, and parallel to what happened in the 1st century seems somehow more interesting.

But my circuits are getting fried, and things start going in one ear and out the other. I begin to think that David is speaking in some tongue other than English. Either that, or I'm not as sobered up from the weekend in Munich as I thought.

The conversation continues for a couple of hours, at which point David announces that we're going to be stopping in Linz to visit with some friends. I'm tempted to get dropped off on the *Autobahn* but this is impractical given the lateness of the hour. In any event, David and Ellen insist that I join them for dinner.

The friends turn out to be more American evangelists. After the initial surprise of having a total stranger join them for dinner, Bob and Ann welcome me into their home. The children go off to play with their local equivalents, and the adults are offered a range of drinks, all of which are devoid of alcohol. The house is furnished simply. Heat comes from a colorful Austrian ceramic stove in the corner of the living room.

We go through some of the 'who are you and how did you get here' stuff. Then the conversation shifts to the business of evangelism and I'm left to observe, which suits me fine.

The discussion of 'business' continues through dinner. I tune in and out, keeping my guard up against any sudden attempt to baptize me in one thing or the other. My cynical wariness proves unnecessary, however. My hosts are nothing but kind, and contrary to expectations, put no pressure on me to do anything other than be a guest.

The words and the laughter of their conversation begin to fade into the background. What I see is a group of people who obviously like each other and sincerely believe in what they're doing. Their relationship seems to be more like a really happy family than any church I have encountered. Friendship, simplicity, a meal together, a life of purpose shared with others. There's something strangely attractive about it all.

But then, they're from Texas.

We finally pile back into the car and arrive in Vienna late at night. David offers to drop me at convenient streetcar stop. As we're retrieving my backpack, he gives me his address and phone number, looks me in the eye and warmly invites me to come to church the following Sunday.

He takes out a prized can of Dr. Pepper and hands it to me. "Promise me you'll come," he says.

I hesitate. At this stage, I feel it would be ungracious to say anything other than yes. I think back to the dinner in Linz and the possibility of belonging to a community made up of people like David and Ellen and their friends who are so inclusive and loving.

A gust of wind whips around us, slapping me in the face with cold rain. 'No,' I think, 'that would be dishonest. I would be compromising my intellectual convictions for the sake of a good meal and friendship.'

I sort of mumble a commitment to come 'sometime, just can't do it in the next week or two'.

David smiles, digs out another can of Dr. Pepper and presses it into my hand. "God bless you," he says.

The streetcar arrives just in time to rescue me. I wave goodbye to David, heave a sigh of relief, and resolve to give up hitchhiking for Lent.

CHAPTER 8
An Unexpected Miracle

Early January, Vienna

"HERR BOCK, WOULD YOU LIKE to have tea with us?"

It was Sunday afternoon, and I was busy unpacking in my newly rented room in *Heiligenkreuzerhof*, located, literally, in the center of Vienna. This is a major improvement over living for the last four months in the suburbs near the *Reichsbrücke*.

My room looks out into a stone paved courtyard. Dating from the late 12th/early 13th century, *Heiligenkreuzerhof* was originally a warehouse and living quarters for the *Heiligenkreuz* (or 'Holy Cross') monastery located on the outskirts of Vienna. It was extensively remodeled in the 18th century and eventually converted to apartments.

My landlady is the wife of a retired professor at the University. My room is off the main entry, across from the bathroom. The Herr Professor and his wife live in a suite of rooms that is separated from the foyer by large paneled double doors. I like the privacy. It means I can come and go without actually disturbing my hosts.

Her invitation to tea on the day I moved in was a terrific way to get established in my new location.

"*Es erfreut mich sehr,*" I reply, 'I would be delighted'.

I've learned that older and well-educated Viennese have a courtly politeness, with proper forms of address. My landlady and her husband are both fluent in English, more so than I am in German. But I feel I can establish some goodwill early on by indicating that I am willing to operate in the local language if they would prefer.

I follow my landlady into the main apartments. The Herr Professor rises to greet me. I guess he's in his 70s, white hair, lean, erect and courtly.

"Good afternoon, Herr Bock. It delights me to meet you. Welcome. Sit down, please."

He gestures towards an overstuffed settee. The Herr Professor takes a chair opposite. His wife returns with tea and sits next to me.

"So, how do you like Vienna?" he asks.

"Very much. I'm enjoying it even more now that I am living inside the Ring."

'The Ring' is short for the *Ringstrasse*, the boulevard that Franz Joseph I built in place of the medieval walls during the mid-19th century. The original walls were built in the 13th century using the ransom paid to release Richard I of England. They were upgraded in the 16th century and were essential in repelling the Turks.

By 1848, the Turks were long gone but domestic revolution was a real risk. Franz Joseph decided to imitate Napoleon both in creating a grand boulevard like those in Paris and in reducing the opportunity for revolutionaries to build barricades. Boulevards make it easier to use canons to control crowds and thus ensure the safety and stability of the Austro-Hungarian Empire. Not to mention the Emperor.

"And is the room satisfactory for you?"

"It suits me very well. It's very light and comfortable. It seems very quiet except for the bell in St. Stephan's."

The professor laughs. "The bell is called the *Pummerin*. I believe it translates as 'Boomer' in English."

"That seems like an appropriate name."

Actually, I think 'Boomer' doesn't quite do it justice. My room opens onto a courtyard, and I can almost see the steeple of *Stephansdom*, St. Stephen's Cathedral, a few streets away. When the *Pummerin* does its booming thing, my room literally vibrates. I try to imagine what it is like in summer when the double windows are open. No sleeping late on Sunday mornings.

"The *Pummerin* is one of the largest bells in the world. The original bell was cast in the late 16th century out of canons that were abandoned by the Turks after the siege of Vienna. That bell was destroyed when *Stephansdom* was set on fire at the end of World War II. The current one made in the early 1950s."

"I had the impression that Vienna was not badly bombed during the war."

"Yes, that is true, except for the time the US Air Force lost its way and bombed the Opera instead of some oil refineries in the suburbs. The damage to *Stephansdom* was caused by an artillery battle at the very end of the war. The German army set up its defenses on the northeast side of the city. But the Russians attacked from the south. The two sides were shooting at each other over the center of the city, and some of the shells fell on St. Stephens. There was no way to control the fire, and everything inside *Stephansdom* that could burn, did."

"The restoration has been very good. It's hard to see any damage today."

"True. But the whole building should have completely collapsed."

"How so?"

"After the war, I was asked to advise on the reconstruction of the cathedral. I was a professor of geology at the University. The government asked me to inspect the foundations of the cathedral to make certain they were not damaged. I had a crew of workers dig a shaft below ground so we could look at the foundations directly. After they had been digging for some time, I realized that they had actually dug *under* the wall. I had them dig in several more places. In each case, the same result. We had to conclude that *Stephansdom* actually has no foundations."

"Then what kept it standing?"

"The walls were actually held in place by the 14th century wooden roof beams. When those beams burned, the walls should have collapsed in on each other. And it would not have been feasible to rebuild the cathedral the way it was originally.

"When the Gothic cathedral was built, the lower walls were built around the Romanesque cathedral that was already there. Then the Romanesque cathedral was taken down and the stone used to build the upper walls of the Gothic cathedral. If the walls had fallen down, one could not reconstruct the cathedral without building proper foundations. And that would have been prohibitively expensive."

"It sounds like a great piece of luck."

The Herr Professor looks at me for a moment, then says gently, with great care, "that it didn't collapse is a miracle."

The way he says it catches me by surprise. I wonder if something is being confused or lost in the translation. The German word *'Wunder'* can be translated either 'wonder' or 'miracle', depending on the context. The Professor could be saying, *'Es ist ein Wunder'*, and mean the same thing that an English speaker would intend with, 'it's a wonder the walls didn't fall in'.

But in German, his word order would put the emphasis on *'Wunder'*. More likely than not, the Herr Professor wants me to understand that he has witnessed a *miracle*, a supernatural event, and that he believes this despite being a geologist with a background in materials science.

'Es ist ein Wunder.' A *Pummerin* of a different kind rings in my head.

"Very interesting," is about all I can muster in response.

The professor's wife senses my consternation and comes to my rescue. "Some more tea, Herr Bock? And have one of these cakes, please." The conversation shifts to other topics and after another very pleasant half hour of conversation, I take my leave to continue unpacking.

Back in my room, I realize I've been a bit naïve about the link between intellectual life and religion. I had *assumed* that any serious intellectual, e.g., university professors, would naturally be atheists or at least agnostics. I wasn't prepared for a geology professor who believes in miracles, partly because geology seems to me to be a science that should produce – and/or attract – atheists. For starters, it completely blows away any literal understanding of 'six days of creation'.

More generally, I guess I was expecting the University of Vienna to be filled with logical positivists. The Herr Professor has unintentionally forced me to reconsider some of my assumptions, including whether and how serious science can coexist with religious belief.

I'm sure there's a good explanation to be had. For now, I'm content to go with the idea that traditional belief in God lingers on in some of the older professors and scientists.

I make a note to read a bit more on the philosophy of science. It's not that science would ever lead one to belief in God. But, maybe the epistemology of scientific understanding is more complex than I think.

CHAPTER 9

Through Spanish Eyes

Early February, Vienna

"DANNY, IT SOUNDS TO ME like you're letting your heart overrule your head."

This afternoon, Danny and I sat for a long time in a coffee house just off *Hoher Markt*, engaged in intense discussion about love and religion.

Danny is generally guarded about his religious background and beliefs. He grew up in the post-Holocaust environment, convinced that the safest thing for Jews is to treat religion as a private matter and to strengthen the separation of church and state. Danny isn't particularly observant, but his Jewish heritage is important to him and he has an undercurrent of disdain and suspicion for Germans.

Today, we're in a deep discussion of religion, this time centered around Maria, the very pretty and very charming Spanish girl that Danny has fallen in love with. Maria is also on the IES course, by the circuitous route of going from Spain to the US for college and then taking a year in Vienna.

Maria gives new meaning to the word vivacious, and it's small wonder that Danny has fallen for her. She's petite, very pretty, with long, dark wavy hair, eyes that sparkle, a wonderful smile and an infectious laugh.

The problem is that Maria is very serious about her Catholic faith, and Danny is trying to relate to her on a spiritual level. I think this is drawing him into troubled water.

"David, you think everything is in the head. Life is more complex than that."

"Danny, our *experience* may be more complex than we can immediately understand, but we still need to try to understand it. We may feel attracted to another person and be tempted to simply call it 'love', but motives and feelings are complex, as you know. I see you going down a path that you simply would not travel were it not for your attraction to Maria."

"So, what's wrong with that? Don't human relationships count at all in your world, David?"

I can tell Danny's a little exasperated by my fairly cynical attitude towards love.

"Danny, they matter a lot. Why do you think I'm sitting here for hours trying to understand what's going on with you and Maria? I'm just wary of the set of emotions people associate with the word 'love', especially between a man and a woman. There's a lot of stuff going on in any such relationship. Better to be driven by your head than some other part of your body."

The waiter drifts by our table to see if we would like something else to eat or drink in addition to the several cups of espresso and pastries that we have consumed.

"*Etwas anderes, meine Herrn?*" 'Something else, gentlemen?'

We're expecting Maria to join us any minute, so we put the waiter off for now.

"Yesterday, Maria and I went into a church together. Maria knelt and prayed. I sat and meditated. But mostly I just wanted to be with her while she prayed. There's something intense and spiritual about her prayer. There's a presence."

"A presence?"

"It's hard to describe. It's not anything visible or audible, more mystical."

"Mystical? Come on, Danny, that's precisely what I've been trying to tell you. And here I thought you were a quintessentially reasonable guy." I smile, more of a smirk actually.

"Okay, you Teutonic potato head. Sometimes in life you just need to be *un*reasonable."

"Ah, Danny, you forget that I'm Swedish. We're talking about Nordic angst, not German rationalism."

We both laugh. Danny is quiet for a minute.

"The thing that really gets me is the way she talks about Jesus. It's as though he were a real person in her life. She's very Catholic – the saints, the Virgin Mary, the rosary and all that. But that's not the key thing for her. It's her relationship with Jesus. Sometimes I think she will end up becoming a nun."

"How does that make you feel?" I remember dating girls who talked about Jesus like he was their (other) boyfriend.

Danny idly stirs the residue in his coffee cup, then looks me in the eye. His expression is serious.

"I'm intrigued. Who is this guy? Why does he have such an impact on people like Maria? There seems to be a big difference between him and what I've experienced from Christians. I'm trying to understand what makes him so special to Maria."

I'm not sure what to make of Danny's response. The first reaction is a slight panic. Danny has been my friend and partner in putting down religion. Now his desire to understand Maria's world has him, a Jew, interested in *Jesus*? Love seems to have done something to his understanding, challenged his prejudices, maybe his convictions.

So does friendship have some of the same power? Might my friendship with Danny pull me along into his reconsideration of Christ through Maria's eyes? The panic meter moves from slight to moderate. Action is required.

'Come on, Danny. You know you can't separate Jesus from Christianity. What we know about the historical Jesus is all filtered through the church, and shaped over centuries to support religious and institutional interests. I'm worried about you. What happened to the skeptical cynic that I used to know?"

"David, the difference between us is that you're an atheist and I'm a skeptic. You take your atheism seriously, so seriously that you're out to convert the rest of the world to your point of view. I'm just skeptical about religious beliefs and very opposed to mixing religion and politics. That's what happens when you get called 'Christ killer' as a kid. But I don't think of religion as the root of all evil."

"Nor do I, Danny. I just think it's untrue, and when people believe untrue things, they are capable of being manipulated for bad ends."

Just then Maria comes through the door, spots us in the back of the coffee house and gives us both a smile that lights up the room. I get up so she can sit down next to Danny. One of our ongoing topics of conversation is flamenco dancing, how it works and what it means. So as I pop up from the table, I go into an ersatz flamenco dance in her honor.

"Look, Maria, I've been practicing."

I bang my heels rapidly on the floor and weave around her with arms alternately above my head and behind my back, snapping my fingers to an imaginary beat. Fortunately, the coffee house is nearly empty. Maria puts her hand over her mouth and doubles over in giggles.

"David, you're perfect." She laughs freely, eyes alight and the energy in her smile is palpable. If her charisma has anything to do with her faith, it would give even an atheist pause.

Danny laughs. The waiter glowers across the room.

"Get of here, David, before you get us all thrown out."

Maria grabs my arm and looks at me with those shining eyes.

"No, no, David. You must stay."

I sigh and give Maria a kiss on the cheek.

"No, Danny's right. I need to be going. I've spent the afternoon trying to rescue Danny from your charms and it's been a complete failure. Besides, I have some studying to do."

As I head for the door, I look back over my shoulder at Danny.

"Keep thinking, Danny."

"Leave it alone, David. Some things, like love, are just to be enjoyed."

CHAPTER 10
Atheist Paradoxes

Late February, Vienna

TONIGHT WAS ONE OF THOSE times in life when life could have gone either way – up or down, forward or backward, onward or simply stopped.

It started out with Danny and I regrouping at the start of the new semester in the *Altes Rathaus* for a cheap *Wienerschnitzel* and beer.

"So, David, how was your break?"

"I went to Athens and Crete. Looked for the Minotaur but couldn't find him."

"No kidding. I went to Greece as well. Ended up at a party with friends of Nikos Kazantzakis. Even met Zorba's sister. How was Crete?"

"You met Zorba the Greek's sister?" Once again, I am amazed at Danny's savoir-faire and ability to connect. It must be the olive skin and Mediterranean features.

"Crete is barren and cold in February. But I met a guy who claimed to be just like Zorba. He conned me into helping him load barrels of olive oil in exchange for a ride from the south side of the island to the ferry in Heraklion."

We both laugh at the contrast between our experiences in Greece.

The waiter brings our food.

"*Mahlzeit, meine Herrn.*"

"*Danke sehr.*"

Another great *Wienerschnitzel* at the *Rathaus*. We drink to life in Greece, Vienna and Europe generally.

"Danny, I've been thinking about our conversation before the break, and your comment about me being an evangelical atheist."

"I don't think I called you evangelical. But you're much more committed to straightening out the world than I am."

"Maybe. My atheism is just a preface."

"A preface to what?"

"That's the question I was asking myself in Greece. When I was sitting on the beach in Crete, I started thinking about why I'm an atheist. I realized that I started out just reacting to the culture around me. So my atheism was partly a matter of being against religion, any religion. My atheism was also a form of rebellion against authority. It set me free to do what I wanted, what I thought was right. I found it very liberating."

"So what's changed?"

"Time and distance, I think. The non-existence of God is a settled fact. But there's a paradox in atheism that I'm starting to see for the first time. At the same time, I see how important religion is to some people. Maria, for example. Religion provides a framework of meaning and purpose, as well as a community joined together by deeply held beliefs.

"Before that, I saw religion as essentially negative, an anachronism to be done away with. Now I see it in a more nuanced way. There are some good aspects mixed in with the bad."

"Really generous of you, David." Danny laughs.

"But, Danny, it's not *true*. Nothing about religion passes a rigorous test of truth. It is, by definition, a matter of faith rather than reason. People believe because they want to believe, not because it's true. They're pandering to their emotions. Or it's some mix of wish fulfillment, projection, fuzzy thinking, delusion and self-deception."

"Okay, okay, I get it! Tell me about your atheist paradox."

I take a sip of beer and fiddle with a *Schwechater* beer mat for a moment.

"It's a paradox of rationality. Atheists are rationalists. They believe that there is a logical, empirical explanation for everything. But one of the facts of life is what Viktor Frankl calls 'Man's Search for Meaning.' We're all looking for meaning for our lives, for significance as human beings, for some purpose to life. And transcendence."

"Transcendence?"

"As I see it, Danny, human beings are the only species that can actually anticipate their own death, from an early age. They live their whole lives, however brief or long, however happy or sad, with the awareness that death will eventually take away everything they care about – the people they love, the things they cherish, their significance as human beings. This awareness gives rise to *Angst* and feelings that there must be more to life than simply 'eat, drink and be merry, for tomorrow we die.'

"I still don't see the paradox."

"The search for meaning is an extension of the scientific belief in a universe that functions according to knowable laws. There is a reason for everything, and given enough time and resources, human beings can understand everything."

"Except the meaning and purpose of life?"

"Exactly. Meaning isn't a scientific concept. It's a religious concept that springs out of the Judeo-Christian belief in a rational universe created by a rational and knowable God. The paradox is that this concept of God and the universe made science possible, but then science undercut the foundational beliefs of western culture."

"So God created science and then science killed God."

"That's one way to put it. Unfortunately, the question of meaning is still with us, like a ghostly echo in the universe. We desire it. We search for it. But now maybe it's just a question without an answer. This is also Camus' paradox. Life is fundamentally meaningless, yet we have to have meaning to make life worth living."

Danny looks at me with an expression of sympathy and concern.

"Ashes to ashes, dust to dust, David."

"Exactly, Danny. Death crowds into the happiest and best moments of our lives. Nothing lasts, nothing endures. And the more we create, the more we love, the greater the loss."

"So isn't death just a fact of life that we have to accept?"

"I think everyone has to find resolution to this fundamental *Angst* of existence. For most people it's some form of religious belief. Christianity is all about getting to heaven, getting eternal life. But it's no longer credible."

"What about Stoicism or Buddhism? Maybe one of the other oriental religions?"

"A lot of people start or end up there, Danny. They strike me as solutions that abandon the rationalist belief system. In those systems of thought, life, consciousness and the universe are mysteries that cannot be understood or comprehended, but only lived with and meditated on. The goal is harmony, acceptance, or resignation, not understanding and control. That's not my world. And to go there seems like a retreat from the struggle for truth based on a rational, logical use of the human mind. I have the same basic problem with the Logical Positivists, who argue that the question of meaning is itself meaningless and thus should be abandoned or ignored."

"So we're not going to solve this problem tonight?" Danny laughs, and it loosens me up.

"Sorry, I'm pretty passionate about this stuff. I want to find the truth about the human condition. Do we just accept the paradox? Is there an answer? If so, what it is?"

"Tomorrow's another day. Speaking of which, I have some studying to do this evening."

Danny and I walk out of the Altes Rathaus and say goodbye. It's snowing lightly. I decide to go for a walk to clear my head.

The Vienna city government makes it easy for people to do self-guided walking tours in the inner city enclosed by the *Ringstrasse*. Buildings with significant historic interest have numbered plaques and flags on them. The numbers correspond to entries in a readily available guidebook that give a short summary about why that particular building is significant. You look for the flags, find the corresponding number in the guidebook, and you can wander the streets and read your way into Viennese history.

In the last six months, I've done this so much that I can do a passable job of tour guide myself.

I grew up in a place where history started in about 1890 so I get a lot of pleasure out of walking the streets of Vienna at all hours of the day and night. For many Viennese, however, history seems to have come to an end after World War I. 'Damals' – 'back then' – is a word you hear a lot in Vienna, and frequently it seems to be referring to the days of the Franz Joseph I – who died in 1916.

But my walk in the snow on this particular wintry night in March isn't for the purpose of exploring Viennese history. It's a peripatetic search for meaning and truth.

CHAPTER 11

In the Grip of Darkness

Late February, Vienna

STUDYING IN VIENNA WAS INTENDED to be a way of broadening my horizons, learning German, steeping myself in European history and culture and advancing my prospective career as a philosopher and writer. Before I started this little adventure in Europe, I really liked the idea that the universe itself makes no moral demands on us. There are no fixed rules, no cosmic laws or external purpose that dictate how I should live. I am free and fully self-determining. It was highly liberating.

Tonight I'm not so sure.

I walk for a couple of hours in the snow, reprising some of the discussion over dinner with Danny. The snow starts to accumulate and drift across the sidewalks. The city becomes eerily quiet. Traffic is light or nonexistent. My mood progressively darkens as I walk, and I begin to be overtaken by a weird kind loneliness that has nothing to do with physical circumstances and everything to do with meaning and significance as a human being.

I begin to realize that I've reached an intellectual impasse. It seems to me that philosophy has no answer to the problem of meaning. Either you forget the question or go in the direction of religion, psychotherapy or hedonism – 'eat, drink and be merry, for tomorrow we die.' But I can't drop it, and I don't like the other solutions because they turn away from the rationality that defines and elevates us as human beings.

My passion for truth is ending up as a cosmic longing for significance. In the absence of a satisfactory answer, it has become a deep and painful cosmic loneliness.

And despair.

The scene in the adventure movie shifts again. The search for El Dorado is taking me through deep jungles of thought and emotion. Having escaped the python, I'm now knee deep in a pit of quicksand. In my case, it's the quicksand of nihilism – no meaning and purpose to life, no difference to being dead or alive. And tonight Camus' solution of accepting the absurdity of human experience and, like Sisyphus, just pushing the boulder back uphill one more time, leaves me cold.

I come to a bridge over the old channel of the Danube, which runs along the north side of the city. I stop in the middle of the bridge and look over the side at the river flowing underneath. A thaw has loosened the ice up-river, and large sections of ice float by in the dark water. The snow is a little heavier now, and the ice rolls in the current. A streetcar rumbles over the bridge, empty except for the driver, conductor and a couple of passengers.

The light of the streetcar temporarily blinds me and it takes a few minutes for my eyes to adjust again to the darkness. As I look down again at the river, the dark water seems to be beckoning me.

Is this the solution to my search for the meaning and purpose of life? Is it here in the Danube, in late February, surrounded by an ice flow?

I know from experience of wading waist deep in an ice-filled river in Idaho that a human being can last only a matter of minutes in such conditions before hypothermia sets in and all resistance to drowning disappears.

The wind has come up and the snow swirls around me. Small drifts move across the bridge. I lean a little further over the wall and listen to the icy water calling me. I watch the ice flowing in the dark river – rolling, sinking and rising again. A kind of gravitational force seems to come over me, a deathly darkness that pulls at the sleeve of my coat and encourages me to just slip over the side of the bridge and put an end to a fruitless quest.

As I stand there listening to the Sirens of Suicide calling to me and wondering if I should just put an end to it all now, I'm suddenly transported back to a time when the thought of suicide seemed so real I could touch it.

My high school disaster occurred sometime in the late fall. I made it through the Christmas holidays by simply shutting down emotionally, something that I had learned to do at the age of 10 when mother died. I was also trying to figure out what to do about college. Then the bad news arrived from Reed College after Christmas, and not long thereafter, as I dropped my girlfriend off at her house after a date, she told me that she wanted to break up.

I could readily see that my self-inflicted humiliation and her decision to break up were not directly connected. I think she just realized that going steady with me was turning into a hellhole. I was too needy and looking for the wrong kind of affirmation from her.

I suppose this would have been a good time to have a mother, someone who could give me a hug and tell me that everything was going to be all right. Not having had much experience with mothers, I don't know if it would have made a difference or not. But that's clearly not the job of a high school girlfriend.

However, the breakup also shattered my emotional lockdown, and the pain and heartbreak were overwhelming. I watched her run up the steps to her house and then drove off in the middle of the winter night, a night very much like this one. I felt I needed to get out of town and headed for a place where I knew I could hang out for a few days – my grandmother's house in Boise.

I drove for a couple of hours in the snow, emotionally overwhelmed and in lots of pain. I began to wonder if I really wanted to go on to Boise or try to find a quicker way out of the pain. On the Interstate, I started focusing on the trucks pushing through the dark and snow in the oncoming lanes. I realized I could end the pain now by driving into one of them head-on. All I needed was a break in the divided lanes, and it would be over.

But I ran out of gas before I could do it, got stuck on the side of the highway, and by the time I got back on the road, it was starting to get light in the east. Things didn't look so bleak in the light of dawn. I drove on to Boise for the weekend, full of resolve to never let myself become so emotionally vulnerable again.

Here on the bridge, in a dialogue with myself, I begin to argue that 'committing suicide in the middle of the night carries the risk that you're letting emotions overtake reason. If suicide is the right option, David, then it needs to be done in the bright light of day – sober, collected and thinking clearly.'

I look up at the snow blowing around the streetlights. Nihilism. Nothing has meaning. There is no difference between being dead or alive. Nothing matters.

Except what you choose.

Tonight I decide to choose life. With a brief salute to Camus and his concept of life's absurdity, I pull my feet out of the quicksand, turn around, and walk off the bridge – back towards *Heiligenkreuzerhof.*

Yes, tomorrow is another day.

CHAPTER 12

Dead End Dialogues

March, Vienna

ONE THING I PICKED UP from Plato was the value of a literary device – the Socratic dialogue – as a way of thinking through complex problems. Socrates had a profound influence on Plato, and Plato returned the compliment by writing down – probably 'reconstructing' – Socrates' way of challenging conventional wisdom, perceptions and flawed reasoning through a process of cross-examination. In short, Socrates forced people to think, sometimes when they didn't want to.

Today, I'm lingering over a double espresso in one of Vienna's many coffee houses and thinking about two other great intellects that challenged orthodoxy and reshaped Western thinking – Darwin and Freud. I'm trying to imagine how they would respond to my persistent questions about meaning and purpose.

I decide to start with Darwin.

'Excuse me, Professor Darwin, I have a minor problem with your theory.'

'What is it, young man?'

'Well, human consciousness is highly evolved, wouldn't you agree?'

'Absolutely. The human brain is the result of millions of years of development. As a species, humans have come to dominate the rest of nature through their large frontal cortex and highly developed powers of reasoning.'

'Would you say that a human being's ability to reflect on, and anticipate, its own mortality is a product of evolution?'

'Yes, of course, young man. How else would it arise?'

'So here's my problem, Professor. That reflective ability sometimes leads to suicidal despair. In fact, since the problem of despair has been known to overtake highly intelligent and artistically gifted people, one could conclude that the more highly evolved you are, the more likely you are to kill yourself. How does that fit with 'survival of the fittest'?'

'It fits perfectly, my dear fellow. Suicide is a way for the human species to rid itself of less vigorous, dysfunctional members. When a human inherits genes that are predisposed to this kind of despair over mortality, it is a good thing that they kill themselves – particularly at a young age – so that this genetic defect is not passed on.'

'But, Professor, many people who embrace your theory most whole-heartedly think that artistic sensitivity and creativity are evidence that survival of the fittest produces progressively better outcomes for the human species. I think it's what we mean by civilization. Moreover, this genetic defect, as you call it, is not simply a piece of psychological dysfunction. It's existential.'

'What do you mean by existential?'

'That it's part of being human. What may have once been a matter of physical survival has become a search for transcendence and meaning. The pursuit of understanding became a pursuit of truth about the world, our place in it, and how to explain this ability to be both part of and yet outside the physical world. The most common answer is the religious one – this is what it means to be created in the image of God.'

Darwin interrupts. 'For goodness sake, young man, you're not going to invoke myth to explain it, are you?'

'No, that's why I came to see you. But so far, it seems that this existential reality doesn't fit your theory. The desire for permanence or transcendence is part of being human. But it's also dysfunctional. If your theory is the final answer to the problems of human existence, then *this cosmic longing is just a cosmic dirty joke.*'

Darwin stares at me for a long moment. I can tell that my 'cosmic dirty joke' comment has irritated him.

'My boy, I see you are obsessed over truth, and it is leading you into suicidal despair. I suggest that you consult with my friend Dr. Freud. I think he should be able to help you with your obsession.'

I knock on a door.

'Dr. Freud? Professor Darwin recommended that I see you.'

'Come in, young man. Yes, Darwin told me about your conversation with him. Lie here on my couch and let's have a little chat. Are you comfortable?'

'As comfortable as one can be on a piece of Viennese period furniture.'

'Your problem is one of repressed sexual desire. The wish for immortality is linked to the evolutionary drive to reproduce. The fact that you are obsessed with transcending your own mortality tells me that you are not expressing these sexual desires adequately. When was the last time you had sex?'

'That's none of your business.'

'Ha! See, your response is proof positive that you are sexually repressed. You need to spend more time in bed with your girlfriend. You do have a girlfriend, don't you?'

'Not at the moment.'

'For God's sake, no wonder you're having problems. It's winter, you're lonely and you're sexually repressed.'

'But Dr. Freud, this isn't some kind of neurosis. It's an existential problem of truth and meaning. The Viennese weather certainly isn't helping. But I have been wrestling with this in good times and bad. Besides, I have a lot of distinguished company in this conversation – Plato, Aristotle, Kant, Hume, Shakespeare, not to mention Sartre and Camus.'

'Tut, tut, young man. I'll be the one to say what a neurosis is and whether you have one. Which you do, by the way.

'But I can help you. My assistant will schedule your next appointment. In the meantime, whenever you have these feelings of anxiety, take one of these little pills.'

At this point, I hear the refrain from a Kingston Trio song playing in my mind: 'Oh, Dr. Freud, oh, Dr. Freud, how I wish you'd been otherwise employed.'

'Hold on just a minute, Doc. I resent being categorized in this way.'

Freud scribbles in his notebook.

'My issue is a real problem in philosophy having to do with what we know, how we know it, and why we know it. The question of transcendence is a long-standing problem. The most common resolution to the issue is some form of religious belief. One could say that it is universal. It is certainly the answer that the vast majority of the world's population embraces.

'But you just define it away by giving it a different label. I admire your creativity, but see it as intellectual sleight of hand.

'As for mental illness, I have some first hand observation of how you and your followers deal with it. Electric shock therapy, hospitalization, endless varieties of therapy, none of which cure anything. It's the moral equivalent of bleeding people. My father spent his life savings on expensive mental hospitals for my mother, and she still died in one.'

Freud keeps taking notes.

'My dear boy, you are very ill. I'm wondering if I need to put *you* in a mental hospital.'

'I'm out of here, Siggie. Call me when you get ready to take my issue seriously.'

Freud throws down his pen in disgust. I slam the door behind me.

Well, so much for that bright idea.

My little exercise in Socratic reasoning quickly turned into a dead end. My imaginary dialogues with Darwin and Freud have not helped advance my quest for the El Dorado of meaning. In fact, they have made things worse as I realize that two of my intellectual heroes might not have a satisfactory answer to this paradox of rationality.

What next? Religion? God forbid!

CHAPTER 13

Italian Sunshine

Easter Sunday, Rome

IT'S EASTER SUNDAY AND I decided to join a hundred thousand or so close friends in St. Peter's Square. Walking into the Square, I realized that Doctor Benesch had again maneuvered me into a religious event.

During the guided tour of the Vatican on Saturday, the Frau Doctor asked me if I'm planning to be in St. Peter's on Sunday. I mumbled something about 'not being interested in a Catholic Mass'. Attendance at Easter Mass is obviously optional, and I'm looking forward to sleeping in, having a late breakfast at a sidewalk cafe in Trastevere and watching the people go by while my earnest Catholic colleagues schlep off to Mass.

Benesch, in her kindly blue-eyed way, is ready for me.

"The Mass is held on the steps of the basilica and you're not like to see it very well. Most people go along for the experience of being there and to receive the Papal blessing."

"Papal blessing? Definitely not my thing."

"But it might be meaningful for one of your friends. After the Mass, the Pope comes to the balcony and blesses everyone in the square. People often bring crosses and medals to the square so the Pope can bless them. You might think about doing that for someone back home. The weather is supposed to be very nice."

She finishes with her best sweet reasonable smile. I immediately think of one of my father's best friends.

In one of the ironies of small town Eastern Idaho, an active Free Mason (my Dad) and the head of the Idaho Knights of Columbus (John Daniher) have developed a close friendship over many years and spend a lot of time together. Dad is not just a Mason. He's also a Shriner and contributes a lot of time to the DeMolays, the Masonic youth group that has, as I remember it, a distinctly anti-Catholic orientation.

But such is the topsy-turvy world of Mormon Territory.

So here I am in the Vatican on Easter Sunday with my newly purchased St. Christopher's medal. We pass through a barrier where we have to show our admission tickets. In the midst of a lot of Italian words I can't readily translate, I see 'Il Papa' in bold lettering. I guess that this is Italian for 'the Pope'.

The square is filling quickly as people converge from all sides. It's easy to keep up with the Catholic students in my group: just look for the girls with small, triangular scarves in Easter egg colors on their heads. I note that the Easter Bunny is conspicuous by his absence, along with colored eggs, chocolate candy rabbits and baby chickens. The Italians have yet to figure out how to turn religious festivals into non-stop commercial circuses, at least here in the heart of the Vatican. I think they're fighting a losing battle. The Easter Bunny's ancestors were here first, in the form of pagan fertility rites. Even the name of the day comes from a pagan goddess.

As I look around the square, however, I don't get the sense that the crowd is at all concerned about pagan influences. It's a sunny day in spring, and there's a festive air about the place. The story of Jesus' resurrection fits naturally with the renewal of life in the physical world.

I wonder: is it because the Italians are culturally more connected to enjoyment of life that they find it easier to believe and participate in a big Easter event? Or is their Catholicism, lightly carried as it might be, the cause of their ability to find satisfaction in good food, wine and time with their friends? Or is it just the Mediterranean climate?

The Pope is an Italian. Nietsche was a German. Is there a connection?

The Mass commences, somewhere out of sight. I'm sure the first 25,000 to arrive have a better view than I, but that's okay. The service is broadcast through loudspeakers, which contributes nothing to my understanding given the quality of the Vatican's public address system. Each phrase echoes around the Square, which I note is actually in the shape of an egg. Hmm… maybe I was wrong about the Easter Bunny.

I look around and study the façade of Michelangelo's architectural masterpiece while the Mass echoes away. At the top, in the center, is a series of statues, one of which I take to be St. Peter. 'So, Peter,' I think, 'what's a nice Jewish boy like you doing in a place like this?' I try to imagine what Peter might think if he could see himself now. Would he be pleased to be perched on top of an ornate building in the former capital of the Roman Empire? Given Jewish scruples about graven images, how would he feel surrounded by 140 statues of various saints, including his Pharisee buddy Paul?

I start to imagine a little dialogue.

'You're a long way from Galilee, Peter.'

'I sure am.'

'Is this what you expected when Jesus said to leave everything and follow him?'

'Not really.'

'What happened?'

'Well, when the Romans found they couldn't crush the early Christians, they decided to co-opt them by making Christianity the state religion.'

'Hmm. I thought that was a good thing. Stopped the persecution, created jobs for all kinds of priests and bishops.'

'It was at first. But then all kinds of pagan stuff were added in. Christmas trees. Easter bunnies. Fancy buildings, elaborate rituals, etc. Men dressed up in fine silk robes with funny hats.'

'Interesting, Peter. Is Jesus still involved?'

'Not really. He got kicked upstairs. Everybody needs to check in with his mother now.'

'Funny, I thought he was a really down to earth guy, you know, a carpenter who had some radical ideas about loving other people.'

'He was. But that's not really satisfying to people with a strong religious bent. They like to be at the center of things and control other people with scary stories and complex arguments about this or that. Frankly, I don't understand the half of it.'

'So this stuff we see around us doesn't really have that much to do with Jesus?'

'Not really. It's basically a system of social control with a large bureaucracy and a big budget.'

'You mean, Marx was right? It's the opium of the masses?'

'Well, I think that's a bit harsh. But you have to dig around a bit to find the good stuff.'

The Mass finishes and a bit later the Pope appears on the balcony in his white robes and bishop's mitre. A great cheer goes up from the crowd. There's lots of waving. 'Il Papa' waves back. It all seems so festive. The cheering dies down, and Il Papa greets the crowd in a variety of languages, including English. Scattered cheers and applause go up when each group of pilgrims hear their own language.

I notice people around me starting to pull out crosses, medals and various other objects. I guess we must be getting close to the blessing part of the morning, so I dig out my St. Christopher's medal and hold it discretely lest anyone see that I'm actively participating in this little event. Finally, Il Papa stretches his arms over the crowd and says something that the Vatican sound system translates into gibberish. But the crowd gets the message. People hold their objects and bow their heads to receive the blessing. I maintain a straightforward gaze at the scarf in front of me.

Il Papa finishes, and there's another great cheer. It's a strangely moving experience, and a smile creeps across my face almost against my will. The sun is shining. It's spring. I'm in Rome. And life is happening.

More than that, life is being *affirmed*. A couple of months ago, I was standing in a very different place, confronting the consequences of a nihilistic philosophy. How close did I come to dying on that snowy bridge? Close enough. But at the last minute, two basic human capacities – memory and story – provided a vine to grab hold of and pull myself out of the quicksand. I chose to live until morning, and it worked.

Now, I'm here in the midst of a vast crowd that seems drawn together in an affirmation of life. It doesn't seem to have much theological or philosophical content, just a human desire for meaning, significance and immortality.

For a brief moment, I am caught up in it. For a brief moment, it doesn't matter if it's true. It's a good feeling, a very good feeling.

CHAPTER 14

Dialog a la Buber

May, Vienna

"*Dona nobis pacem. Dona nobis pacem. Dona nobis pacem.*"

AS WE DROVE BACK FROM Sunday Mass, the four children, ages three to twelve, were singing '*Dona Nobis Pacem*' in the form of a round. The day was warm enough to have the sliding roof open as the VW bus chugged up *Hohenstrasse* into the Vienna Woods, where Clarence and Alberta live. The children sang the complex harmony of the canon perfectly, and it felt like a scene out of the Sound of Music. I half expected to run into Julie Andrews around the next corner.

Clarence is the Dean of Students for the Vienna IES program. He is also a professional artist and the art instructor. Over the last several months, Clarence and Alberta have progressively incorporated me into their family life with invitations to dinner, long walks in the woods, family outings and many hours of conversation about life, love, friendship, art and spirituality. I'm spending this weekend with them. They offered to let me sleep in on Sunday morning, but I opted to go to Mass with them at the local Catholic Church.

Clarence and Alberta grew up on neighboring farms in Indiana, married and came to Vienna in the 1950s as students on the first

IES program. My first encounter with Clarence was in the IES office, shortly after coming to Vienna. The dominant impression was of someone who is right there with you, in the moment. A warm smile, lots of energy, eyes that dance and seem to look into your soul. Something clicked.

We turn off *Hohenstrasse* into a small meadow called *Sulzwiese* that contains several buildings including an *Eldersheim*, a retirement home. Clarence and Alberta's apartment occupies the top floor and attic of one of the buildings. Alberta turns to the task of cooking breakfast. The family typically fasts before Mass, and this morning I elected to join them. Not, of course, because I had any intention (or would have been allowed) to take communion, but 'when in Rome...'

"So who would like some *Slivovitz*?"

I look at Alberta to see if she's serious. Alberta is tall, slender, dark hair and dark, expressive eyes that simultaneously convey fun and compassion. She smiles at me. "Austrians believe that it enhances digestion," she says sweetly. "I'm not so sure. But it certainly does get you going on a cold morning."

Clarence appears with a bottle of *Slivovitz*, hands us each a shot glass and pours.

"*Prosit!*"

I down my glass, and fiery plum brandy burns all the way to my toes. Once again, life with Clarence and Alberta is expanding my horizons. Fasting, Mass, *Slivovitz*, bacon and eggs – to paraphrase Dorothy, 'Toto, I've got a feeling we're not in Idaho anymore'.

After breakfast, Clarence and I go for a walk.

The Wienerwald contains an extensive network of well-maintained hiking trails. We strike off in the direction of *Kahlenberg*. Along the way, Clarence points out places where the family has gathered wild mushrooms and entertains me with a story of collecting and cooking snails from the forest. The conversation naturally flows into a discussion of art and nature. Clarence is also an encourager of my own creative side as the faculty adviser for a student journal called *Dialog*. In addition to contributing a couple of short stories, I'm also helping edit this year's edition.

Clarence is an interesting and complex friend. Here's an Indiana farm boy who studied at the Chicago Art Institute, migrated to Austria, mentors young artists and writers, has a wife and four kids, is a cradle Catholic and outwardly lives a very conventional life. A deeply thoughtful and sensitive man, his vision of friendship is equally deep and challenging. Martin Buber looms large as an influence, and Clarence has given me a copy of Buber's *I and Thou*. In Clarence's world, friendship consists of sometimes just being together and not necessarily doing things. Silence is something to be cherished rather than felt awkward about. And conversation involves more than words, something Buber talks about in his book *Dialog*.

"Clarence, I was looking at the painting next to your easel last night, the one with the face in it. Is there a story to it?"

It's hard for me to fit Clarence's work into familiar categories, but I've learned that most of his paintings are *about* something. He reads widely, thinks about life, meaning, purpose, friendship, death and dying, nature, and spirituality. And he seeks to express his thoughts and feelings in his art. I suspect that the painting in his studio is a self-portrait of sorts. It's abstract, oil on canvas, in earth tones, and impressionistic. The overall effect is a pattern of sections much like an irregular stone floor, with a face in the center.

"*Immer.* Always." Clarence makes a dramatic sigh and laughs, the self-deprecating humor indicating that life and art is serious business, too serious to take oneself all that seriously.

"It's part of a series of paintings I did on a Man of Sorrows theme from Isaiah."

"As in Handel's Messiah?"

"Similar. Christians generally apply Isaiah 53 exclusively to Christ. I see it as a broader theme, the result of seeing and taking on other people's sorrows, being with them in their grief. It takes lots of forms, but at the heart of it is a willingness to become involved in people's lives and thus vulnerable to their pain and sorrow."

Clarence turns to me as we walk along, and I look back at him. The expression on his face is like the painting, a mixture of deep caring tinged with sorrow. I look away, and we walk in silence for a while.

"And what about the style? Is there a story there, too?"

"I call it my stones and bones phase. It was triggered by an experience several years ago. A friend of ours who is an Austrian priest asked us if we would be interested in seeing what was in the crypt of his church. The crypt had been sealed off for as long as anyone could remember, and the Diocese had decided to open it up to create more space. It was all a bit mysterious, since no one knew why it the crypt had been sealed in the first place."

"Sounds fascinating. What did it turn out to be?"

"The crypt had gothic arches that had been walled up with bricks and plaster. Alberta and I were there when the workmen broke through the walls. When we shined a light into the opening, the crypt was full of human skeletons. Apparently, during a plague or epidemic there were simply too many bodies to bury, so the church began simply stacking them in the crypt and sealing them off."

I stop walking, and Clarence does as well. We stand on the path, not saying anything. I hear the birds singing, and feel the warm spring sunshine. I try to imagine the scene.

"It must have been shocking."

"It was very powerful, too much to take in. I remember the effect of seeing all these bodies piled on top of each other, mostly just skeletons against the stone floor and walls of the crypt. Eventually, I began to use some of those images in my painting as a way of processing what I had experienced. In the Man of Sorrows paintings, I try to express the connection between man and nature, life and death, and the stone and bone style is intended to capture the feelings and experience of sorrow."

"Is that why you did the painting of *Mariazell?*"

Also hanging in Clarence's studio is an abstract landscape of *Mariazell.* The cathedral is in the center surrounded by the mountains and the village. The colors are rich greens, blues, browns and reds. The painting is impressionistic – tiny sections of color separated by faint black outlines. Up close, it loses definition. But at a distance of several feet, you see the entire mosaic. You also see that the dividing lines are mostly in the form of crosses.

"No, I did that much earlier. *Mariazell* was a family outing. The whole scene inside the cathedral was just so dominated by crosses. It gave me the idea to weave the cross theme into the bigger landscape. I did a lot of paintings in that style. I keep that one to remind me that I had to stop painting like that or I was going to go blind."

Another laugh.

I think back to my own weekend in *Mariazell*. "I've been doing some processing of my own." I tell Clarence the story of the Ancient Austrian and then about the night I came close to jumping off a bridge. Clarence listens without comment other than the silent understanding and compassion in his face.

"What got you off the bridge?"

"Still thinking. Still believing that there is an answer to Camus' paradox. Not ready to give up yet."

"I'm glad to hear that." Clarence looks at me and laughs, but his expression fleetingly looks like the face in the painting. "And I'm glad you didn't jump."

"Me too."

Later, Clarence drives me down to the Grinzing *Strassenbahn* station. On the way, I tell him about my experience at Maria Laach.

"I'm still trying to figure out what happened there. I agreed to stay in the Vespers service for 5 minutes and ended up rooted to the floor. And then I didn't want to leave. I had this profound sense of *longing*. For what I'm not sure. God, maybe? Whatever it was, it was deep, and I couldn't make sense of it.

"Now, it's sort of like an old war wound where the bullet is still somewhere in my body, and the experience keeps getting reawakened at odd times. Like Maria Zell or Rome. Or in conversations with friends."

I look at Clarence, who keeps his eyes on the approaching switchback. "Does it *mean* something? Am I supposed to *do* something with it?"

We arrive at the station. Clarence pulls into a parking spot and turns off the engine.

"Sometimes deep spiritual experiences are showing us something about ourselves. Sometimes there are desires that run too deep for words."

We sit quietly in the bus for a minute or so.

"Is this what Catholics mean by a calling to the priesthood?"

I blurt the question out before I can stop myself. I'm not sure where the question comes from. Clarence looks at me, obviously bemused by the question, searching for a thoughtful answer.

"I'm probably not the right person to ask. But it could be something that you might want to explore. I can suggest some people you might want to talk to. My brother Vince is a priest who works as an editor for a religious publisher. He's coming for a visit next month. You might want to come out and meet him."

An unguarded comment now seems to have taken on a life of its own. I open the car door.

"Sure, why not? I would love to meet Vince. Thanks again for a great weekend, Clarence. *Wiedersehn.*"

"I enjoyed it. *Wiedershaun.*"

On the streetcar back to the Ring, a deep sense of irony overtakes me.

I think back to the confrontation with a Catholic priest in Salt Lake City and the way I cut him off in his attempt to engage me in a spiritual conversation. I found it funny at the time. But now I'm not laughing. In fact, I'm the one seeking the conversation.

It strikes me that truth is like a tightrope walk. You lean too far one way and you fall into nothingness. Lean too far the other way and you fall into what? Being? Religion? Or just *life*?

The streetcar pulls into the station on the Ring. As I walk back to *Heiligenkreutzerhof*, I realize that I've now wandered into Scene 3 of the adventure movie. Having escaped the python and survived the quicksand, I'm standing in the middle of the dry riverbed trying to figure out which way to go. Not clear, and there are no road signs. But I guess that's what makes it an adventure.

The Mystery of Maria Laach rattled my atheist convictions. If there were a God, I guess Maria Laach would be the place where he threw down the gauntlet. 'You don't think I exist? Let's see how you handle a medieval vespers service? Or a trip to the Alps on All Saints Day? How about a Pentecostal evangelist? Or a beautiful Spanish girl? Try a sunny day in Rome. Maybe you should experience a bit of life with a Catholic family in the Vienna Woods.' And so forth.

But I *like* my atheist viewpoint. It's intellectually satisfying. It sets me free. And it's still the only game in town from the standpoint of reason and logic. And, candidly, it makes me feel superior to the benighted religious types around me.

Unfortunately, it's also deeply unsatisfying as an answer to some gut level questions of meaning, purpose and personal significance. It's just, well, sterile. It lacks power to inspire unless you make it a cause in itself, and then you're finding meaning in a cause rather than in something that is objectively true.

I survey the riverbed, the jungle around me, the mountains on all sides. Upstream or downstream? Something tells me I need to go up, away from the quicksand, but still keep a wary eye out for the python.

CHAPTER 15
Salinger and Newman

Mid October, Vienna

IT'S THE START OF A new academic year and I'm still in Vienna, now on a full scholarship as a Dean's Assistant in the IES program. I realize that this is likely to stretch out my undergraduate career, but believe that the extra year in Vienna will be worth it. I can improve my German, pursue some advanced subjects in philosophy and deepen my friendship with Clarence and Alberta. Clarence is an amazing mentor in life, and working with him in his shepherding the IES students is terrific opportunity.

I spent the summer working for the US Army at a base in Dachau. Yup, *that* Dachau. The concentration camp is gone, but the adjoining SS base has a small French army unit (it's their sector of Germany) and a much larger US Army unit. It was my first and hopefully only experience working in a commercial scale laundry, but it provided fuel for my 10-year-old VW, some needed spending money in Vienna, and some interesting excursions in Germany.

Today, I was back at Clarence and Alberta's house, this time invited to a reception in honor of a Catholic priest (Father Walsh) who is writing a book about Salinger. When Clarence invited me, he explained that Walsh is a good friend of J.D. Salinger and had come to Vienna to do research for his book.

Clarence's brother Vince is Walsh's editor. When Vince visited in the early summer, I had a chance to spend some time quizzing him about Catholicism and what made him decide to be a priest. We had a good, but inconclusive discussion. Vince later sent me a book on Catholic theology, which helped me understand what Catholics believe without moving the needle in terms of my own set of issues and questions about faith vs. reason.

The apartment is warm and inviting though crowded on a somewhat grey Sunday in October. I'm enjoying a robust red wine from the Neusiedlersee area east of Vienna. I know a few people besides Clarence and Alberta, mostly IES students and faculty. Most of the guests are Catholic literary types. And, it's a new experience to be part of an international literary event, especially one connected with Salinger.

I turn from a conversation with one of the IES faculty to see Walsh headed in my direction. I take a step back, thinking he's aiming for someone on the other side of the room, when he reaches out to shake my hand and introduces himself as John Walsh. By his accent, I'm guessing he's Boston Irish. He's medium build, graying hair, friendly, affable and ready to talk.

I introduce myself and then ask Walsh, "What brings you to Vienna?" The question is disingenuous. I know why he's here, but it's the best I can think of.

"I'm doing research for a book on Salinger. He lived in Vienna in the late 1930s and I'm trying to fill in some details of that period."

We chat for a bit about Salinger, how Walsh knows him and his reclusive nature. We also talk about Walsh's other work for the Catholic

Church. Having a conversation with Walsh is easy. He's a great storyteller and full of interesting insights. But then he directs the conversation towards me.

"I understand that you have some questions about the faith."

I nearly choke on my wine and see why he sought me out. I feel awkward, but also flattered by his interest. Someone, probably a combination of Vince and Clarence, must have told him about my interest in things Catholic.

"Well, yes, I'm doing some reading and thinking. Vienna is full of new things for a kid from the potato fields of Idaho. Roman Catholicism is one of them."

Walsh laughs at the potato reference. "Have you read Newman's Apologia?"

"No, I haven't." Actually, I've never heard of Newman, nor can I quickly figure out what an 'epi-loge-e-a' might be about.

"You should read it," Walsh says with considerable enthusiasm. "Newman was a brilliant guy and writes very well. Give me your address, and I'll send you a copy."

I clear my throat. "That would be very nice. Maybe the easiest thing is if you send it to me care of Clarence at his office."

"Great! I have Clarence's address. I'll send it when I get back to the States. I think you'll like it."

"Thanks. I look forward to reading it."

Walsh moves off to chat with other people. I'm left trying to figure out what just happened. Here's a Catholic priest who is a friend of JD Salinger and who has taken at least a passing interest in my philosophical quest and promised to send me a book. I begin to realize that Catholicism is not just another church but a country unto itself. I make a mental note to find out who Newman is.

An hour or so later, Walsh leaves to head back into Vienna. The crowd thins out, but there is still a lot of lively conversation. I look around the room and spot yet another priest, one I happen to know, so I edge over to have a chat with him.

Monsignor Ungar is the head of Caritas but lives in an apartment in the *Eldersheim*. He says Mass most Sundays at the *Eldersheim* but also pastors the English speaking Catholic congregation that meets inside the Ring, something he started doing after World War II. Ungar looks to be in his mid-50s but his hair is white. His glasses give him a scholarly air, particularly when puffing on his ubiquitous pipe. He comes across as a kind and modest man, and very approachable. I've had a couple of discussions with Ungar about Catholicism.

"*Grüss Gott*, Monsignor. Nice to see you again. Everything well with you?"

"Yes, everything is fine. How are your explorations going?"

"Well, thank you. They're continuing on a number of fronts. Still lots of questions about the nature of faith and the role of sacraments."

Ungar doesn't immediately respond. He looks pensive and, for what seems like a long moment, says nothing.

"Some people say that the first time they take communion, the host tastes incredibly sweet."

I watch Ungar's face, waiting for him to continue. I'm guessing he's talking about his personal experience. He just looks at me thoughtfully. Finally, I break the silence.

"But getting to communion in the Catholic Church requires a commitment to the Church, which itself is an act of faith."

"Yes it does. That's the essential first step."

"I guess I'm still trying to work out what one needs to know prior to making that step."

"I can see that."

At this point, someone comes over to speak to Ungar and the conversation shifts. I wander away, bemused by Ungar's response. Walsh was keen to push me along in the Catholic direction, Ungar seems relaxed, almost diffident about it. No pressure, take it or leave it. At the same time – as near as I can tell – there's no easing into Catholicism, no place to dip one's toe in and test the water.

All or nothing, your money *and* your life.

And once again, I find the whole process frustrating.

There's a scene in the movie *Barabbas* – the fictional story about the thief (more likely, revolutionary) whom Pilate released instead of Jesus. Barabbas goes back to his wicked ways but is unable to escape the influence of the Galilean who ended up on Barabbas' cross. He ends up in Rome, and when he hears (mistakenly) that the Christians are setting fire to the city, he grabs a torch and finally throws in his lot with Jesus, only to be stopped by a Christian who tells him that this is not the way of Christ. Barabbas has a look of total bewilderment and says, 'Why can't God make himself plain?'

Indeed, Barabbas, why can't God make himself plain? Why all this movement in shadows? Why this need for a humiliating and perverse 'leap of faith'?

This seems like a preposterous way to order your life, particularly when the requirements of the Christian life are so onerous. So why jump into it? Surely, it seems to me, the more demanding the course of action you choose, the more important it is that it be done rationally and with the fullest possible knowledge of the alternatives and their consequences. Right?

I guess I will wait to see what Newman has to say. In the meantime, I think I prefer my skeptical position to the sudden embrace of an arduous life for the sake of an uncertain gain — even if it may be 'incredibly sweet.'

CHAPTER 16

The Navy Pilot and the Priest

Late November, Vienna

I WENT TO CHURCH TODAY. Actually, I just went *into* a church, the *Jesuitenkirche*, which just around the corner from the *Heiligenkreuzerhof*. It's an incredibly ornate church, almost over the top, in High Baroque/Rococo style. There was a lot to look at while I was contemplating the future of the universe.

I sat there for a while trying to imagine what a conversation with God would be like, sort of man to man. The trouble is that it isn't man to man. I guess one of the privileges of being God is that you don't have to talk.

The point of my visit was to imagine a dialogue with God as a way of processing a set of philosophical issues that have emerged since my fateful question to Clarence and the subsequent events that it generated. Unfortunately, I didn't get very far, other than God's saying 'Hello, nice to see you again, but please sit further back,' or 'What are *you* doing here?'

Mostly, God maintained an inscrutable silence.

Dialogue with Jesus was equally frustrating. He seems to have only one answer to all questions:

'What's the meaning and purpose of life, Jesus?'

'Come, follow me.'

'What's it like up there on that cross, Jesus?'

'Come, follow me.'

'How can anyone possibly live according to the Sermon on the Mount?'

'Come, follow me.'

'How's the weather today, Jesus?'

'Come, follow me.'

'Will you please stop with the "come follow me" stuff?

'Come, follow me.'

And so it goes. The God dialogues are just not working for me.

I did spend a fair amount of time contemplating the 'over the top' interior of the *Jesuitenkirche,* particularly the twisted green marble columns. They seemed to fit neatly into the jungle adventure movie. Close my eyes and I could almost see the python wrapped around one of them.

I also spent some time studying one of the many crucifixes in the *Jesuitenkirche* and reflecting on a conversation with Clarence about the man of sorrows.

As I look at the figure of Christ on the cross, am I seeing the Lamb of God who suffers for the sins of the world, as the Mass says? Or the Man of Sorrows who suffers with me? Is the cross just a symbol of human failure and evil? Or is it about the compassion of Jesus for his friends? Am I supposed to feel guilty when I look at Jesus on the cross? Or comforted? Both at the same time? If so, how?

It seems to me that Christianity has more than its share of paradoxes.

A dominant one for me is that you can't follow Jesus without embracing the Sermon on the Mount with all of its perfectionist demands. But if you're honest about it, it seems clear that it can't be done. As a result, embracing Jesus' message will inevitably lead either to hypocrisy or to frustration, failure and disappointment. Why do it?

A further paradox begins to take shape in my mind.

Following Jesus involves major sacrifice, as he himself repeatedly reminds his little band of disciples. Take up your cross, deny yourself, be prepared to die for what you believe, leave family and home to live for others, etc. It would be foolish, therefore, to attempt to be a Christian without being totally committed. You need to embrace what the Catholics call the counsels of perfection – which to my mind appears to require one to be a priest or nun.

Bizarrely, I find myself analyzing the decision whether to embrace Christianity by looking past the idea of simply becoming a Christian to deciding whether and how such a decision brings in issues of career and vocation and not (just) a particular set of beliefs. In short, can I see myself as a Catholic priest, and if so, why? What would it involve? And how would it scratch my itch for meaning and significance as well as knowledge and truth?

Here I realize I need to tread very carefully. I can tell than I'm involved in a search for self-definition. Who am I? Not, who am I right this minute? But who am I *meant* to be? Who do I *want* to be? What are the criteria for making such a decision?

Sartre poses this as the challenge of freedom: we're free to choose. But freedom is only freedom in making choices. Not to choose, or to deceive ourselves into believing that we are not fully free and fully responsible, is bad faith. For Sartre, there is nothing or no one that we are *meant* to be. We are, or become, what we choose.

It's easy to look at an institution like the Catholic Church and say, 'this is where I belong, this is what gives me an identity.' In other words, we sacrifice or invest our freedom into an institutional structure that returns the compliment by affirming our significance. But life then becomes a flight *from* freedom by seeking and accepting the judgment of others about our personal worth.

After my freshman year of college, I wandered into the Navy recruiter's office in Idaho Falls. I took a bunch of tests, the results of which qualified me for just about any job in the Navy (or so the recruiter said).

But there was only one job I was interested in: being a fighter pilot. I was attracted to the technical challenge of landing a jet fighter on a carrier deck, the potential for life or death combat, and my romantic image of adventure at sea. In other words, it fit my value system like a glove.

Unfortunately, the recruiter's tests also showed that I was partially red-green colorblind. And thus ended my dream of being a Navy fighter pilot.

I would have done it gladly, partly out of small town Idaho patriotism, but also because I thought of Navy pilots as elite and heroic. The sacrifices of the Navy life seemed small by comparison.

The parallels between the Navy and the Catholic priesthood are not particularly obvious but I think I see some common themes. Both involve sacrificing your own self-interest for something larger than yourself, forsaking the comforts of home and family in order to help others, and defining your personal identity in terms of the role and history of a large and enduring organization.

The big difference is that being a Navy pilot sounded like a terrific ego boost. Being a priest is, well, not so attractive in this regard.

For obvious reasons, I don't have a Catholic (or Christian) set of values. And I wouldn't be sitting here thinking about this if it weren't for the experience at Maria Laach and the inclusive nature of my Catholic friends in Vienna. That painful longing, the awakening of some strange cosmic desire, still lingers in my life, a bit like the lingering smell of incense here in the *Jesuitenkirche*.

A German phrase from the Mass keeps rattling through my head – '*Erbarme Dich unser*'.

Strange though it may seem, I've never been to a Mass in English, only German. My impression from the German is that it involves a lot of breast-beating, pleading and groveling. The Catholic God seems to be an irascible sort of guy, demanding of humans what they can't provide, namely moral perfection. So the tenor of the Mass is, 'I'm a really, really, miserable failure, so please, please have mercy on me.' I have enough trouble with my own perfectionist tendencies without embracing a perfectionist God.

Of all the phrases in the Mass, '*Erbarme Dich unser*' is the one that is stuck in my head. 'Have mercy on us,' in English.

By itself, it's not a bad sort of prayer. You don't have to buy into the idea of complete and total personal failure to recognize the benefits of a little mercy from time to time. Perversely, because I'm not a Catholic and German is not my native language, I can say it on my own terms, without all the baggage of the Mass. Or even a belief in God. It sort of counts as a prayer, absent the commitment that might be required if I said the same thing in English.

'*Erbarme Dich unser.* Anyone there?'

Once again, God is silent. I'm alone with my thoughts and paradoxes in the *Jesuitenkirche*, except for Jesus' annoying 'Come, follow me.'

Note to self: try spending less time in churches.

CHAPTER 17

Switching Sides

Christmas Eve, Zell am See

"SO, ARE YOU GOING TO translate for us?"

Katy's question is sincere but betrays a lack of understanding of how a Mass works, not to mention my German language skills.

It's Christmas Eve and I'm sitting with a group of students in the *Heiliger Hyppolit Kirche* waiting for midnight Mass to begin.

I've discovered that being a Dean's Assistant is a mix of information bureau, tour guide, fixer, big brother and translator. Many of the students have less than a semester of German, and they want to follow a Catholic Mass in German if possible.

This is especially true for the Protestant students, who have little clue how a Mass works. Since this particular group includes Katy, a girl I've been dating who is an evangelical Christian, I assume that I can get by with some general instruction about the Mass, rather than simultaneous translation.

"I think you will find the Mass easy to follow. The church is accustomed to having lots of foreign tourists here on Christmas Eve. The carols and homily will be in German. But I suggest that you not focus on understanding all the words but on the overall effect. After all, Catholics successfully suffered through the Latin Mass for centuries and hardly understood a word of it."

I wink just to make sure everyone is tracking. The girls laugh.

Once again, the irony of the situation amuses me. I probably have less religious background than any of the other students. This is certainly true with respect to Katy, a fun-loving girl from the Northwest who saw *The Sound of Music* and fell in love with Austria – or at least Julie Andrews. She is an enthusiastic tourist and insisted we stop at *Oberndorf* so she could take a picture of the church where Silent Night was composed.

Besides, I have a personal interest in just absorbing the scene. After a year and a half in Austria, I have gained an understanding of European culture, including a much better understanding of Roman Catholicism. In one sense, it's highly intellectual. But in another, Catholics seek and try to create an *experience* of God. The atheist in me says this is just superstition and emotionalism.

But as Danny said, some experiences need to be left alone, unanalyzed, absorbed and accepted for what they are. Maybe there is something existential about a Christmas Eve mass. Maybe it touches a basic human need for transcendence, for contact with something 'spiritual', for something 'mystical.'

By itself, Christmas always provokes thought and reflection. The idea of a God who cares and gives is touching all on its own.

Sure, I could break this all down into its psychological components and its relation to ancient myths and religious practices in cultures that know little of the Christmas story and care less. But tonight I'm in a mood to just enjoy it, to listen to the music, smell the incense, hold a candle and enter into the story.

The Dean's Assistant translator is off duty. As is the philosophy major.

The Mass is everything I hoped it would be – pageantry, music, ceremony, things to touch all the senses. It recreates some part of the feelings from Maria Laach, that mysterious longing that is hard to put into words. The homily is short and uninspired, but sticks to the key message of Christmas. I have a wonderful time and lose track of the group of students with me.

After the Mass, Katy and I walk back through the snow to our hotels. A group of French teenagers walk quietly a little bit ahead of us. I can't help noticing the effect of the service on kids who during the day seem to go out of their way to be annoying. Yes, there is something special about Christmas Eve.

"So, Katy, what did you think?"

"I thought it was really, really beautiful. I really liked the candles and the music. But I thought the whole priest thing was overdone. And it was like they were trying to create barriers between the people and Jesus."

I'm a little unprepared for Katy's response.

"In what way?"

"By not letting everyone take communion. I think communion is for anyone who believes in Jesus."

I feel my Christmas goodwill rapidly dissipating.

"Well, the Catholics have a different view. And, as we're in Austria and taking advantage of the opportunity to attend a midnight Mass in a Catholic Church, we might just have to let them do things their way."

The sarcasm is hard to miss, and Katy looks at me like I am the Grinch that just stole Christmas.

"I don't understand why you're defending them," she says with more than a touch of anger in her voice. "After all, I thought you didn't believe in anything."

We arrive at Katy's hotel, stiffly wish each other Merry Christmas with a short kiss, and say good night. I watch Katy go up the steps and through the door and then continue the walk to my hotel.

I realize Katy has a point. Mellowed though I may be, I'm still officially an atheist and all of a sudden I'm defending the *bête noire* of the Western world. How did this happen?

My first thought is that it was the sort of mystical mood I was in. I really didn't want to get into an intellectual conversation about whose theology is correct. While true, that's only part of it.

Probably more important is the loyalty factor. Basically all of my friends are Catholics, and I'm kind of a fellow traveler, as Lenin would say. Not really a believer or member but sympathizer to the extent that, if I have to take sides in the Catholic-Protestant debate, I am likely to come down on the side of the Catholics. After all, they were there first and the rest of Christianity broke off from Catholicism in one way or another.

I start to say to myself that 'they're the real thing.' But the humor of the situation overtakes me. A year and a half ago, I was slamming a Catholic priest while wearing a Coca-Cola badge that said, well, 'It's the real thing.' Had it occurred to me then, I would have said that atheism is the real thing. Now, in working through whether there is any validity to the Christian faith, I'm focused on Roman Catholicism.

The real irony of the tiff with Katy is that she doesn't know the half of it. I've never said anything about trying to discern if I have some kind of 'call' to the priesthood. At some point, I'm going to have to figure this out, but I expect that Katy will be long gone by then.

CHAPTER 18

Arrivederci, Jesus

Easter, Rome

I'M STANDING IN A COURTYARD inside the walls of the North American College in the Vatican.

"The good news is that I've made arrangements to borrow a Vespa so we can run out to the Pope's summer palace. The bad news is that you have to drive. At least as long as we're inside the city limits of Rome."

Peter gives me a big smile. I'm not sure whether he is kidding about my having to drive a motor scooter through the streets of Rome or not. Peter is dressed in a full-length black cassock and round, wide brimmed black hat worn by seminarians in Rome.

"I'm not allowed to drive a motor vehicle within the city limits. You just have to get us to edge of town, and then I can take over. In the meantime, I have to stay in uniform."

Peter is not quite what I was expecting.

Clarence and Alberta have arranged for us to meet. Peter is from the Midwest, a bright guy on the fast track within the Catholic Church. I'm not sure where he is in the ordination process but he has been selected to do an advanced degree in Rome.

He's perfectly mid-western, lanky, tall, sandy hair and glasses, full of energy with a long stride like the farm boy he once was. Strongly masculine and active, he looks like he would be more comfortable in blue jeans driving a tractor than studying theology in a cassock. The folksy charm and adventuresome spirit is infectious.

Sure, why not drive a Vespa through the streets of Rome with a lanky priest on the back?

Peter walks over to a corner of the courtyard and pushes the Vespa back to where I'm standing.

"Have you had any experience on a motor scooter?"

"Some." This is an overstatement. I once spent an afternoon running around on a Moped restocking Coca Cola concession stands during a parade.

Peter is unconvinced by my answer.

"So, then, let's let you practice a bit inside the courtyard. Jump on."

Peter shows me how the gearshift and throttle work, then kicks the starter and the Vespa revs up.

"OK, just drive around the courtyard a bit to get the feel for it."

The courtyard of the college has a cobble stone pavement. The main gate is a solid metal affair that rolls back to admit motor vehicles. I let the clutch out slowly and head in the direction of the (closed) gate. I'm not going fast, but suddenly realize I don't know where the brakes are. Before I can figure it out, the Vespa runs into the gate, and I come to an abrupt halt, fortunately with no damage to the Vespa or myself.

Undeterred, Peter comes over and gets me turned around.

"Just do a couple of circles in the courtyard and we'll be good to go."

I admire his faith. The Italian security guards appear to be less certain and open the gate.

After a couple of laps in the courtyard demonstrating some proficiency with the brakes, Peter climbs on the back of the scooter and off we go.

I can't resist smiling at the comic quality of the scene, like something out of an Italian movie. A completely inexperienced Vespa driver with a priest in full cassock and sombrero as a passenger, maneuvering through a Roman sea of scooters without the benefit of traffic lights and very few signs – which in any event are all in Italian.

The Italian men seem to drive as if their manhood is at stake, staring me down in intersections and in merging traffic. The women are not a lot different, but they combine it with a wonderful haughtiness intended to make you feel not only incompetent as a driver but also beneath the notice as any self-respecting Italian woman.

Peter knows the way – generally – and every few minutes hails someone and asks in passable Italian for directions. We zip and dart around squares and circles, and I get an occasional glance at pretty girls. I've never wished for a red light before, but it would be nice to stop and take in the scene. Unfortunately, such self-indulgence is likely to come at a high price, so I keep my eyes on the road and about two thousand other Vespas.

In about 20 minutes we reach the city limits, and Peter directs me to pull over. Peter jumps off the back, strips off his cassock and hat and stuffs them in the compartment under the seat. I think we're both relieved. Clearly, Peter feels much better being in control.

In another 20 minutes or so, we stop at a small market and Peter buys bread, cheese, wine, water and some olives for lunch. We head into hills above the Castel Grandolfo, park the Vespa and walk up to a hill with a view over the Papal palace and the lake. It's a spectacular scene in the warm spring sunshine. The Renaissance popes certainly knew how to take care of themselves.

We find a dry spot of grass, Peter opens the wine, says a short blessing, and we begin what has to be one of the most charming picnics of my life.

Peter is gracious, unassuming and straightforward. We talk about our personal backgrounds, interests, families, etc. – anything but religion. He is the sort of guy I would want as a friend, anywhere.

Finally, we turn to the religion issue.

"Tell me a bit about why you came to see me. All I know from a mutual friend of Clarence and Alberta is that you're doing a lot of thinking about vocation and faith."

"Vocation would be a bit misleading. What I'm trying to do is figure out whether Christianity is true. A couple of years ago I was a committed atheist. Then I had an experience in a monastery in Germany that starting me thinking."

I tell Peter about Maria Laach.

"Sounds like a Damascus Road experience to me."

Peter's comment brings back a memory of my Dad reading the story of Paul's conversion to my brother and me one Easter Sunday. He'd found the story in the magazine supplement to the local Idaho newspaper. I always like listening to Dad read; he had a strong voice and he could be very convincing. The story made an indelible impression on me.

"Maybe a weak form thereof. Paul saw a light and heard a voice. I just caught a glimpse of something mysterious."

Peter smiles. "So then what happened?"

"Well, I walked out of the Abbey pretty confused. These things are not supposed to happen to atheists. It started me on a search to find out if there is in fact any truth in the Christian story. As it happens, most of this search has taken place in and around Roman Catholics, notably Clarence and Alberta. And to make the whole thing more complicated, I began asking whether the Maria Laach experience was a calling of some sort."

"As in a calling to the priesthood?"

"Maybe. I really don't have an intellectual framework in which to fit something like Maria Laach. But as it happened in a Catholic monastery, it seems natural to try to understand it within a Catholic framework."

"Interesting. Any conclusions so far?"

"Some. I think I've come to the conclusion that if you're going to be a Christian, you might as well do it whole hog, which probably means being a Catholic. I'm attracted to the idea of historical continuity and authority embedded in Catholicism, as well as the intellectual strength of Catholic thought."

"We call that the Magisterium."

'Magisterium' – great word, I think. Need to remember it.

"I guess I also see the Christianity issue as one of commitment to a way of life as well as to truth. If Christianity is true, then it seems to me that you need to embrace what Jesus says in the Sermon on the Mount. I see no way to do this authentically and honestly other than in a total commitment to his way."

"The Church calls it the counsels of perfection."

"So I've heard. And as I understand it, that inevitably takes you into becoming a Catholic priest. Catholic because that's where you find the strongest claims to Christian authority and authenticity. And a priest because it's a full embrace of the counsels of perfection."

Peter pulls up a blade of spring grass and chews on the end of it, quietly thinking and staring off over the lake towards the palace, the beautiful Italian countryside stretching out behind him. It occurs to me that you can take the boy out of the farm but you can't take the farm out of the boy.

"It seems to me that at some point you're going to have to make a choice."

I pull up a blade of grass and chew for a minute.

"I see it more as a search for truth. Choices are many in life, and they need to be as carefully researched and reasoned as possible. If Christianity is true, then its demands and sacrifices are probably reasonable. But it's not true, then it strikes me as a foolish waste of life. At least, it would be for me."

Peter and I look at each other, each waiting for the other to continue. Finally, I decide to break the silence.

"Tell me why you decided to be a priest."

Peter pulls up another, longer blade of grass.

"Well, I grew up Catholic and had some terrific priests who really cared for their parishioners. They seemed incredibly fulfilled, and if they thought they were making a sacrifice to be a priest, they never showed it. I see it as an opportunity to serve other people, to lead them into Christ and to sustain them in their faith."

"But couldn't you do the same things without being a priest? Or even a Christian?"

Peter looks me in the eye.

"Sure you could, but why? The Christian faith itself is a calling to serve others, to love them as Christ loved us. You don't have to be a priest. But priests play a special role in incorporating people into the body of Christ through the sacraments and being their pastor in Christ's name. It's a calling to follow Christ in a life of sacrifice."

Peter says this gently, warmly and with a quiet enthusiasm. I feel like I've just taken a swift uppercut to the chin. He waits for me to respond.

"What about celibacy? You seem like a red-blooded American boy. Aren't you interested in having a wife and children?"

"That's a tough question. You have to pray for the grace to deal with a vow of celibacy. Love can take different forms, David. The love between a man and a woman is a beautiful thing, as is the love between parents and children. I see the life of a priest not in terms of giving up on love but in committing to a larger, holy love for the people whom God loves so lavishly in Christ."

I swallow hard as Peter says this.

"And what about dealing with your sexual desires?"

"That's all part of the deal. Again, you have to have the grace to deal with it."

We sit for a long time, saying nothing, looking over the lake and gardens. Finally, I look at my watch and announce that it's time for me to be getting back to my student assistant duties. We pack up the lunch remains and head back to the Vespa.

This time, Peter starts off as driver. The wind and the traffic noise make conversation impossible on the Vespa. On the way back to Rome, I think about the conversation with Peter and its implications.

I start to feel like I have hiked up from the dry riverbed to the crest of a hill, looked over the other side and realized that El Dorado isn't there – just a large village with neat, well-ordered streets and tidy houses. No pythons or quicksand but not much adventure either.

Slowly, I begin to see why the life of a priest is not for me. Although I like the idea of being a leader, I still don't see why Christianity is true. Magisterium or not, we're still dealing with fallible human beings and a self-preserving institution. To call it the 'body of Christ' is fine, as long as you mean something other than the institution itself.

More fundamentally, I can't see how I could ever be happy in a life of celibacy. The hormones are just way too strong. Besides, not really having experienced family life, I look forward to getting married some day and having a family of my own. I simply can't relate to Peter's concept of love. It's as though his relationship to Christ is enough for him, it satisfies whatever need he has to be loved and provides his model of what it is to love others – unselfishly and in a sacrificial way. But it is in every way a bridge too far for me.

I also realize that my Idaho roots have imbued me with the frontier spirit – a desire for adventure and freedom. The thought of surrendering my life to the authority of a large bureaucracy fills me with horror. Some might feel secure and fulfilled in such a setting. I can only see myself being suffocated.

That frontier mentality had a lot to do with my becoming an atheist. I wanted to throw off the oppressive culture of small Mormon towns and find my own sense of meaning and significance. I wanted to be free, and that freedom is inseparable from a freedom of thought about basic truth.

Paradoxically, I remember the lettering on the wall of the Christian Science Church that we attended in Idaho: "You shall know the truth, and the truth shall set you free." That idea took root in me and any thought of Christ is bound up with it. It always seemed to me to be one of the most significant things Jesus said.

In the end, the goal has to be truth and freedom, not tradition, security, reliance on authority or sacraments.

A wave of sadness comes over me. I'm disappointed to have come to this conclusion. As Peter said, being a priest could carry with it a very meaningful and satisfying life, living close to the ideal set out by Jesus. But I can't do it.

And so an incipient dream dies like a stillborn child.

Peter and I do the swap again at the city limits. Peter pulls out his hat and cassock and is transformed back into official seminarian. With another, less amateurish navigation of the Rome traffic on my part, we arrive safely back at the North American College, and my chauffeur duties come to an end.

"Peter, it's been a wonderful afternoon, and I really appreciate the conversation. Sorry if I seemed a bit aggressive at times. This stuff has been gnawing at me for a long time and I'm keen to find an answer."

Peter laughs. "I can see that. Where do you go after Rome?

"Up to Florence."

"Let me check my schedule. I could probably jump on the train and meet you up there. We could continue the conversation, maybe with a little tour of Tuscany thrown in."

I'm torn. On the one hand, I would enjoy spending more time with Peter, and I can see the pastoral side of him kicking in. He really cares and is willing to, well, sacrifice if there's a chance of getting me 'incorporated into the body of Christ'.

But I also sense that I am crossing another bridge, this one away from the idea of being a priest and maybe even away from Christianity and Roman Catholicism. I'm hoping that his schedule will not permit an excursion to Florence.

I reach out to shake his hand. "I'll be staying at the Hotel Caravaggio."

"Ciao, David. See you in Florence."

I walk out of the North American College, leaving more than just Peter behind.

CHAPTER 19

The Reluctant Atheist

Advent, Seattle

"So, how is the Advent program coming?"

I'm studying in the living room of the Newman Center just off the University of Washington campus. My inquisitor is an English Jesuit named Roger who has been assigned to the Center for a month as part of his final year of training.

I look up and smile at Roger.

"My bit is easy. It's the others who bear the heavy weight of expectations."

Roger is an incredibly nice guy. Kind, thoughtful, very intelligent and well educated, refined British accent and a good balance of English reserve and friendliness.

"Someone told me that you were organizing the whole program. They said it was your idea."

"They're just establishing who gets the blame in case it flops."

I smile, Roger chuckles.

"Yeah, it was my idea. I saw the Campus Crusade guys' Santa Claus posters and thought there should be something for Catholics. We're just doing a collection of readings and meditations. I'm doing Nietzsche."

"Nietzsche? For Advent? Seems a bit unusual."

"Ah, precisely the point. Nietzsche's atheism was wrapped up with his conclusion that European culture had gutted the message of Jesus. So I'm trying to illustrate what 'before Christ' would look like to someone like Nietzsche."

I'm living in the Newman Center because it's very convenient to campus, it's cheap, and it's largely self-governing. It's also a way for me to continue a low-level connection with Catholicism while I process my experience in Vienna and try to integrate it with my past and future in the US.

The Catholics I have met through the Newman Center all seem to be doing interesting things academically but wear their Catholicism lightly. I went on a retreat with them in the fall and participated in a way appropriate to me. I've been open about my non-committal relationship to Christianity in general and Catholicism in particular.

The Center is under the supervision of a local Dominican parish, so we get periodic visits from the Dominicans. The visiting Jesuits are temporary help, one of whom is a physicist who works at the Jet Propulsion Lab in his spare time. It makes for an interesting and diverse set of conversations.

Roger is obviously intrigued by my choice of material for an Advent meditation.

"Interesting," he says. "How did you get involved with Nietzsche's writings?"

"I did a lot of work on Existentialism a couple of years ago. I found Nietzsche interesting because he relentlessly pursued the consequences of his atheism. But ultimately, he's nihilistic, and I've also experienced the darkness of that way of thinking. It's that feeling of darkness that I want to try to convey in the Advent program.

"By the way, I had a professor in Vienna who incorporated Nietzsche into a course on modern European philosophy. He was English, a former Jesuit by the name of Edward Mowatt."

"Ted Mowatt? Really? Ted was at Heythrop College when I was there. Caused quite a stir when he left the Order. Very nice man, and greatly respected. I recall he had a special interest in Wittgenstein."

I'm startled by this small world encounter. Mowatt was an inspiring teacher who was always available for a cup of coffee and ongoing discussion about philosophy and any other subject you cared to bring up. I knew he had been a Jesuit, but thought he had dropped out at a low level.

"We did a lot on Wittgenstein in his course. He also taught a superb course on Greek moral philosophy."

"Well, good luck. Sorry I will miss it, but I'm due back in California at the end of the week."

"Thanks, Roger."

Roger wanders off to the kitchen for a cup of coffee and gets engaged in conversation with some of the other students who hang out at the Center. I watch this from a distance and begin to realize that the life of a priest is pretty ordinary after all. Apart from the collar, the life-long vows and the mystical nature of the Mass, they could just be bachelors who teach, counsel, write, 'marry and bury' and pastor congregations.

In short, they seem to be living practical lives, making sincere efforts to imitate Christ but not in the perfectionist way I imagined was required or possible.

When I went to Vienna, I was on a quest for knowledge and truth within the framework of a post-Christian secular culture – El Dorado, as I imagined it from Utah. Somewhere along the way – Maria Laach, a bridge on the Danube River – it became a quest for meaning and purpose. And then through a peculiar set of encounters and circumstances, it became a quest about Roman Catholicism and the priesthood. And that quest effectively ended last Easter on a Vespa ride through the streets of Rome.

I feel more settled in the conclusion I reached at that time. I'm not cut out to be a priest. I also realize that my 'Catholic phase' is coming to an end as well. Being in Europe, in Austria, around the traditions and beliefs of Roman Catholicism, challenged me to rethink my values and beliefs. It may be the real thing in terms of Christianity. But you still have to embrace Christianity to become a Roman Catholic.

In the end, however, it still requires a leap of faith. Even if you strip the history and culture of Christianity down to its essentials, it is not rational in the same sense that physics or biology is. It may have its own internal logic, its *Magisterium*, but it is not based on empirically verifiable propositions.

At one time, I could not understand why anyone would want to make that leap of faith.

In my pre-Vienna experience, Christianity seemed like signing up for a life of drudgery, condemnation and hypocrisy. Having been around Catholics for a couple of years, I see more of its appeal – the community, the sanctity of human life, the art and music and culture in its rituals. And then there's the sense of meaning and purpose that I witnessed in Peter, laying down his personal desires and interests in order to create a better life for others and sustain them in their faith.

'Not bad,' I think, 'not bad at all.' If only it were *true*.

Vienna also helped me see the near-inseparability of Western civilization and Christianity. It *is* the moral and spiritual framework for Western culture. If you could some way simply unplug the Church from society, what kind of society would you be left with? Would it still be compassionate, concerned with fairness and justice for the poor? Would it still be broadly democratic, seeing people as citizens with inalienable rights granted by their creator? Would you still be able to appeal to the principles of brotherly love to resolve disputes and formulate policy? I doubt it.

And there is really no answer to Nietzsche: 'Nothing is true, everything is permitted', including the acquisition and exercise of power over other human beings. Nietzsche's 'superman' is the logical – or honest – replacement for the Judeo-Christian social framework in the West. God help us.

Which means that a lot of the wind has gone out of my philosophical sails. And, if my mission in life isn't to replace religion as a framework for society, what should it be?

Another paradox of atheism takes shape. I see the value of religion, but I don't believe it's true. I would like a world in which there is unifying belief system that can produce a fair and just society based on shared values. While I can't get there personally, I now appreciate the fact that a majority of my fellow citizens can.

I would like the outcome to be different. But Christianity remains a bridge too far for me. It's too demanding. And reaching the level of conviction or belief necessary to make the requisite sacrifices is not intellectually possible, at least not for me. I'm not into leaps of faith, which is where a reason-based exploration of Christianity always seems to end up.

Maria Laach is more that two years into the past and a continent, if not a lifetime, away. Its lingering effect on my life is that I'm not the same passionate, evangelical atheist I once was. I think I've mellowed into the 'religion may be alright for you, just not for me' mode.

If I'm really honest about it, it's gone further than that. I have become what you might call a *reluctant atheist*.

Come to think of it, I'm probably not such a bad guy to organize an Advent program. You could characterize my relationship to Christ as 'stuck in Advent.' I never make it to Christmas.

Part Two

CHAPTER 20

Pigs Fly

December, Idaho Falls

"SO WHAT EXACTLY IS A Rhodes Scholarship? And what do you have to do to get one?"

After finishing the term at UW, I went back to Idaho Falls to see my Dad, who was – as he described it – 'over the moon' about the fact that I had won a Rhodes Scholarship. I let him drag me around town to see his friends, and I spoke at his office Christmas party. One evening, one of Dad's close friends asked the questions that lots of people in Idaho Falls probably wondered about but were afraid to ask.

As I think about how to answer Jack's questions without sounding like a pompous ass, I realize how far I have traveled since high school. Not just in miles or experience, but in future prospects. In my senior year, I really had screwed up an otherwise promising and fun high school track record. And, as far as most people in Idaho Falls knew, that's where it ended. Somehow, four years later, everything has changed. Jack's question is a good one – in effect, 'what happened to *you*?'

I decide to start with the easy bit.

"It's a scholarship for graduate study at Oxford, for two years and sometimes three. The trust that pays the bills was set up by Cecil Rhodes who made a couple of fortunes in diamonds and gold in South Africa in the 19th century.

"Rhodes' original goal was to bring American and German students to Oxford as a way of forging personal relationships between the future leaders of the three countries that he thought would be the global powers in the 20th century. He saw the scholarships as a way of reducing the risks of war between England, Germany and the US. "

"That worked out well, didn't it?" Jack laughs and Dad chuckles along with him. I smile, sort of.

"Rhodes probably had the right idea, just a bit late. The Germans got kicked out of the program during World War I. But the American Rhodes scholarships have most likely made a significant contribution to the relationship between the US and England."

"Don't you have to be some kind of super athlete to get one as well as be really smart?""

"Not always. Smart is more necessary than fast. Rhodes was after people who were what he called 'all-rounders with a bulge'. The scholar-athlete image developed because Rhodes wanted people who were physically active and had demonstrated leadership qualities. The All-Americans make the headlines, but most scholars qualify for other reasons."

"So what are you going to study?"

"Well, like many Rhodes Scholars, I've signed up to do PPE – philosophy, politics and economics. But mostly I'm interested in economics."

"You didn't tell me how you got the scholarship."

"Ah, yes. That remains somewhat of a mystery. The process probably played to my strengths more than most graduate school scholarships. The selection criteria are broad and the process includes multiple rounds of interviews, at least eight recommendations and a longish essay on why you think you would benefit from Oxford and what you would do afterwards."

"And?"

"And what?"

"And, how did you do it?"

"Dumb luck, probably. I first heard about the Rhodes in high school and was reminded of it when I went to Vienna. A couple of months ago, I saw a poster on the UW campus inviting applications for the Rhodes. My first reaction was that the Rhodes seemed like a long shot, but hey, why not? They can't say no if you don't ask.

"So I filled out the application, made it through the screening process, then the first round of interviews at the UW level. I went to Boise in early December for the state level interviews and to my amazement made into the regional finals. The rest, as they say, is history."

Jack is quiet for a moment. But I know him well enough to know that he's relentless. He's a bookkeeper by trade and he likes to see that things add up correctly.

"So why do you think they selected you?"

I take a deep breath.

"Strangely enough, I'm guessing it had something to do with working my way through college, including two years in Vienna. Based on the interviews themselves, the selection committees apparently thought my principal sport of lifting cases of Coca-Cola and a bit of skiing were enough in the athletic department.

"The wandering student thing, though, meant that I had recommendations from professors at three universities, the IES Dean of Students, the head of the Fulbright Program in Austria and the Vice Chancellor of the University of Vienna, as well as the Coca-Cola bottler here in Idaho Falls. I guess I made reasonably good impressions on both the academic and business worlds. And I think it gave me something worthwhile to say in the essay. I tried to draw out why I had chosen to do college the way I did and how it has shaped my thinking and approach to life.

"Then there's my capacity for talking my way into and out of places. Somebody told me that one of the members of the Idaho state selection committee described me – meaning it as a compliment – as 'the best bullshitter they ever had'."

Jack starts laughing. "That apple sure didn't fall far from the tree."

It takes Dad a moment to get the joke, and then he starts laughing as well. I'm the last to get it, and it produces a warm father-son moment. Yeah, we are alike in many ways.

I also begin to see that the Rhodes is a bit of redemption for Dad as well. He had the challenge of raising two sons on his own, both of whom he was extremely proud of. It hurt him a lot when I fell from grace in high school, and now he's bursting his buttons to show that the school administration made a big mistake in how they handled my stupid prank.

Jack still isn't finished. "So what's the mystery?"

I have to think for a minute. I'm not quite sure why I used the word 'mystery'.

"Jack, maybe I used the wrong word. It's not so much a mystery as a miracle. It was a very long shot, but everything just seemed to come together in the right way."

Jack nods. Dad, who is somewhat of a believer in miracles, has a pensive look. Just then, Jack's wife announces that dinner is ready and the conversation shifts to other things, to my great relief.

Over dinner, my thoughts drift back to the Benson Hotel in Portland where the final interviews took place. My first interview of the day was a disaster. I arrived in Portland the night before with a bad cold and terrible congestion from the flight. I took a bunch of cold medications to fight the congestion, and the next morning I couldn't think straight. It was a bunch of lawyers, professors and business executives against a very befuddled interviewee.

The second interview, on the other hand, couldn't have gone better. By the afternoon, the medication had worn off, and I was firing on all cylinders. I came out of the interview with the satisfaction that I'd given it my best shot and if I didn't get the scholarship, it would be because it's going to someone who was better qualified than I am.

When the chairman of the selection committee announced that the committee had made its selections, I was tense but also strangely at peace about the outcome. It was one of those moments in life that you never forget:

"The committee has selected the following four men from the Northwest Region to be Rhodes Scholars at Oxford: Bock, Marlantes, Price and Stocking. Congratulations, gentlemen."

The chairman went on to say deservedly nice things about all of the candidates. I didn't really hear that part. I was lost in some surreal world where impossible things happen, dreams come true, and pigs fly. I'm headed back to study in Europe, this time in my dream location. These things just don't happen to kids from small towns in Idaho that screw up their lives at critical points in time.

Yeah, it's a miracle all right. And I plan to make the most of it.

CHAPTER 21

Love and its Complications

Christmas, Bogus Basin, Idaho

OKAY, OKAY, AS IF THE Rhodes Scholarship were not enough, life has taken yet another quantum leap in the space of a month.

After visiting Dad in Idaho Falls, I went back to Boise for Christmas at the invitation of Carl and his friends, including a very pretty girl named Pam. Between Christmas and New Year's, life quickly got complicated — largely because of Pam.

I met Pam when I came to Boise for the state-level Rhodes interviews earlier in December. Actually, I met her mother first, on the flight down from Seattle.

I wasn't particularly surprised when the stewardess asked me if I had a brother named Carl. But I was surprised when she told me there was a woman in First Class who wanted me to come up and sit with her.

I look at the stewardess with disbelief. "It's alright" she says, "there's an empty seat," as if my concern was about United Airlines' policy on who gets to sit in First Class. I gather my stuff and head up the aisle, where I meet a woman with light brown hair, a big smile, and a very firm handshake.

"Hi. I'm Joanna Maitland, and I'm a friend of your brother." Mystery solved.

Joanna also seemed to have unusual influence on United Airlines and immediately orders champagne for both of us. It turns out that Carl knew Joanna would be on the same flight and thought it would be fun to 'set me up'. Joanna and I chat about her business, UW, whom she knows in Seattle, the Rhodes process and what I plan to do in life. It was an easy flowing conversation, aided by United's ample supply of champagne.

My first sight of Pam was at bottom of the stairs at the Boise airport, as she and Carl greeted Joanna and me in our slight, champagne-induced buzz.

After Christmas Pam and I went skiing together. Actually, Pam drove her younger sister and cousin up to Bogus Basin one evening, which boasts the longest lighted ski run in the world, and I tagged along thinking it would give me a chance to get to know her better and maybe show off a bit on the slopes. Unfortunately, I started out looking like an idiot.

Pam and I were in the ski lift line together, and Pam's little sister and her cousin were one position ahead of us. Concerned that the two girls didn't look particularly proficient, I started yelling instructions.

"Reach back for the chair, keep your tips up, and remember to pull the safety bar down!"

Unfortunately, I forgot to look back myself and the chair hit me in the back of the legs and nearly knocked me down. I managed to grab the chair and hoist myself awkwardly into place, narrowly escaping the ignominy of forcing the whole lift shut down to let me get on.

Pam watched me settle in and pulled the safety bar down – slowly. "I thought you were an expert skier," she says with a sly smile.

I give her a sideways look.

"I am. I'm just not a chair lift expert. Usually, I hike up."

Pam laughs, and we settle in next to each other for the ride to the top of Bogus Basin, a ski resort 14 miles up the mountain from Boise. It's early evening and I'm about to experience a 'first' – night skiing on what is billed as the world's longest lighted ski run.

Pam is a smart, beautiful girl with dark hair, classical features, wonderfully warm hazel eyes, a big smile, a great laugh and a sophisticated style.

Pam and I are both keeping our eyes on the girls in the chair ahead. "So how was Idaho Falls?" she asks.

'Pretty much the same as ever. Friendly people, most of whom were totally bemused about the Rhodes Scholarship. I think my friends are pleased for me. I'm glad I came back to Boise for Christmas, however. I'm having fun meeting people. I think your daughter is really cute, by the way. She seems a bit shy but there's also something mischievous about her."

"She can be a real imp. She spends a lot of time at babysitters and with my Mom and sister, but I think she's very sweet."

Pam was once married to my brother's best friend, but is now a single mother coping with the challenges of supporting herself and her daughter as the administrator of a Rockefeller-funded political think-tank in Boise. I felt an immediate attraction to Pam, but quickly learned that she has a number of suitors, one of whom is best friends with her aunt and uncle. There is the prospect of one or the other of these guys proposing to Pam in the not too distant future. So tonight's ski trip is, well, just a ski trip.

As we head up the hill, I begin remembering some earlier Christmases in Boise. I was about the age of Pam's daughter when my mother was recovering from her first 'nervous breakdown.' She decided to move back to her mother's house in Boise and took me with her, and the two of us lived with grandmother Lucy for a couple of years.

I remember Lucy baking and cooking for weeks before Christmas, then packing up large boxes of fudge, divinity, cookies, and fruitcakes to send to friends and family. It was her way of doing Christmas, together with Mamie, a large black woman who had cooked for lots of well-to-do Boise families and spent her final years being cared for by my grandmother.

Later, after mother died, Dad, Carl and I traveled to Boise for Christmas in order to maintain some contact with grandmother and the Ruick family traditions. Grandmother's large, Victorian house close to downtown was a place of adventure.

My grandfather – always 'Mr. Ruick' to Lucy – had been a prominent attorney but died when mother was very young. Inflation and depression depleted the value of his life insurance payout, so Lucy and her three daughters moved into the back of house and rented out the elegantly paneled bedrooms in the front.

Many of the memories in Boise were about adventures in grandmother's attic and other happy times. Some were not so great. This Christmas is definitely in the happy column.

After the first run, we leave the girls to do their thing, and Pam and I spend the rest of the evening skiing together. We talk on the chair lift, on the way down the mountain, digging out after falls, and in warm-up breaks in the lodge. Despite my better judgment I can't help flirting with this beautiful girl with the big smile, particularly when she falls and I swoop down like Sir Galahad to help her up.

We ski for a couple of hours, then head back down to Boise for a late dinner at Joanna's. On the way back to Lucy's house, I feel something stirring inside. Something is going on between Pam and me.

Over the next few days, we see a lot of each other, always with other people around. We have drinks together downtown with her aunt and uncle and some of their political friends, including one of Pam's suitors, dinners with Joanna and Carl and Joanna's current boyfriend and sitting around talking during the day with various relatives, friends and likely future members of my Idaho network.

One afternoon, I suggest another ski trip to Bogus Basin. Pam immediately takes me up on it, and somehow no one else can make it.

Which leaves us on the mountain by ourselves.

This time we ski until the lift shuts down for the night. On the drive down, we stop at a bar that advertises authentic *Gluehwein* – just the prop I need to tell Pam stories about skiing in the Austrian Alps. The bar is dark and intimate and the two of us get into deep conversation about all manner of things. I keep reminding myself that she's spoken for and I am only here for the Christmas holidays. After the New Year, I have to get back to Seattle to finish my degree at UW.

Around midnight, we head back to Joanna's where Pam is picking up her daughter.

I pull into Joanna's driveway, turn off the car and look over at Pam, whom I notice is sitting closer to me than to the door. By this stage, the effect of the *Guehwein* and a great evening together have shredded my better judgment. I put my arm on the seat behind Pam and lean over to kiss her, like a teenager on a first date who's not sure if the girl is going to kiss him back.

My lips are about a centimeter away from Pam's when the thought occurs to me, 'this could get very complicated.'

The complications are numerous.

First, riding into town and sweeping up the prettiest girl around is probably not the right way to start off a new phase of my career. Especially when the girl is the ex-wife of my brother's best friend, the 'ex' wants to get back together with the girl, and I'm not sure what's going on in my brother's head now that he and Lydia are divorced.

On top of that, the family ties between Pam's ex and me go way back. Our grandfathers were law partners, our widowed grandmothers live next door to each other in Boise and our parents have known each other since they first got married.

And then there's my prior (and repeated) resolution not to allow myself to become emotionally vulnerable to yet another girl with whom I will probably fail to sustain a long-term relationship.

Not to mention that I'm on my way to England in the fall, blocked from getting married until after the first year in Oxford, in the process of figuring out what I'm going to do in life and have a negative net worth. As for Pam, she's busy being a responsible, independent, self-supporting single mother and doesn't need the complication of a relationship with a distant graduate student when she has the opportunity to marry someone who can take care of her and her daughter.

Wisdom and common sense suggest that the last thing I should do is get into a romantic relationship with Pam. But like the moth to the flame, I can't resist, and she isn't exactly discouraging me.

Our lips touch, and a slender arm wraps around my neck. I move my hand down onto Pam's back, and I feel the warmth of her skin under the cashmere sweater. Then Pam's big smile turns into the most amazing, engulfing kiss — sweet, warm and electrifying. We look at each other. Those hazel eyes are shining. I feel a surge of desire and realize that Cupid has launched a whole quiver full of arrows at me.

We kiss again. And again. And again.

'This is so out of control,' I think. 'And complicated.'

CHAPTER 22

Choices

Late February, Boise

"YOU REALLY KNOW HOW TO celebrate Washington's Birthday."

Pam and I were having breakfast at a restaurant on Capitol Boulevard. Her Aunt Edie spotted us in a booth on her way out and decided to tease me a bit about how much time I'm spending in Boise.

The University of Washington, like other state agencies, observes Washington's Birthday as a holiday. This year, it lands mid-week. I flew down from Seattle the preceding Friday with the intention of flying back on Tuesday. I met Aunt Edie over the weekend, and she knew that I had stretched the weekend to spend more time with Pam. But Tuesday came and went, and I'm still in Boise on the following Friday morning.

"I've got it covered. UW is opening a satellite campus in Boise." Aunt Edie gives me a wry smile and a knowing look.

I've lost count of how many weekends I've spent in Boise since Christmas or the hours on the phone with Pam. Our conversations range across all manner of subjects – music, art, politics, philosophy, etc. Today, our conversation drifts inadvertently onto the subject of religion.

"So how does Edie fit into your family?"

"She's the twin sister of Uncle Richard, Hope's husband."

Richard is a prominent trial attorney in Boise. Hope is active in Idaho and national politics. They're both helping me find a summer internship in the state government. Pam's parents divorced when she was in high school. I know next to nothing about her father, who died a few years ago.

"I see. I thought there were a bunch of aunts on your mother's side."

"There are. Mom's the oldest, then there's a brother named King, then Miriam, Banjo, Grace and Hope."

"Banjo. Interesting name."

"Short for Evangeline. Grandmother was serious about religion and gave her children Biblical names. Except for her son, who got her maiden name. Granny was a King, related in some way to the King Ranch people. She died a couple of years ago. I sometimes traveled with her in the summers when she would go on tour as a preacher and evangelist."

A cloud appears on the horizon. Pam and I have been too busy exploring other things to talk about religion. Now, I suddenly realize that I'm having breakfast with the granddaughter of an evangelist. I'm not too worried because none of her relatives seems to be religious other than in the most conventional sort of way. No hang-ups about alcohol or sex. Good Episcopalians as near as I can tell.

Still, I feel a need to probe a bit, particularly given the subject that I really want to discuss this morning.

"What kind of evangelist was she?"

"I actually don't know much about what she believed. My father was very conventional when it came to religion. He made Granny promise never to discuss the subject with me or to take me into any of her meetings.

"Granny and I drove across the country one summer, staying with people she knew. She would go preach in a local church or tent meeting, and I would stay with her friends. I was her first granddaughter, so I probably got lots of prayer."

"How long did she do this?"

"Most of her life. She had some kind of religious experience as a teenager. She was apparently very pretty and had a great singing voice. She had an opportunity to go to Hollywood, but gave her life to Jesus, as they say. She married an Iowa farmer, had six kids and did her evangelism thing. Mom was the oldest, so she was the one who basically raised the younger kids."

"Interesting. So did anyone follow in your grandmother's footsteps?"

Pam laughs.

"Hardly. In fact, most of the children went completely the other way. There are lots of wild stories I could tell you. Banjo was an artist, married another artist. Grace married an Army officer. King is working on his second or third marriage. Miriam is probably the most conventional. She's married to an Air Force officer and has five sons. Mom and Dad divorced a few years before he died."

"What happened with your parents?"

"It's a long story. Mom thinks they were never well suited. Dad grew up in Montclair, New Jersey, went to Brown. Wealthy family from what I understand. But his father died when he was in college, and he broke all ties with his family after his mother remarried too soon, in his view.

"At some point, Dad canoed his way down the Mississippi and met Uncle King in Iowa, who introduced him to Mom. After World War II, they moved to Jackson, Miss, then to Idaho because Dad liked to hunt and fish. He traveled a lot and eventually drank a lot. They split when I was in high school."

"That must have been hard on you."

"It certainly didn't help. But my problems are basically self-inflicted."

As Pam says this, I see again the maturity and resiliency that I find so attractive about her. Pam's life hasn't been easy, but she gives no hint of self-pity or an inclination to blame others for the slings and arrows of outrageous fortune. Besides being pretty, she's kind, self-sufficient, affectionate, and fun to be with.

While we haven't known each other very long, I have the sense that Pam is the first girl I have dated who seems able to deal with my intensity without being either frustrated or overwhelmed – no mean feat, in my view. I think it's because she has such remarkable people skills – her kindness and thoughtfulness enables her to tease me out of my over-intensity without making me feel put down or judged.

So, reassured on the religion front, I press on with this morning's plan of action.

"I'm looking forward to spending the summer here in Boise."

"So am I." Pam says this with a big smile and a warm laugh.

"So what would you think about coming with me to England in the fall?"

Pam laughs. "What exactly are you proposing?"

Her question catches me a little unprepared. I was trying to ease into a discussion about a long-term relationship. Her question is a little ambiguous, but has a sharp point – like an arrow in my chest.

It would be nice to just move to Boise and keep dating Pam with a view to eventually marrying her. Unfortunately, I don't have that option. I can't get married until after the first year at Oxford. And Pam has other options, including moving to Seattle with her mother in the fall. I don't want to run the risk of losing her.

Flash to the waterfall scene of the adventure movie. The hero is paddling his canoe down a big river. He hears a waterfall up ahead and knows he should quickly head for shore. The river starts to move faster, the hero hesitates. Then he realizes it's too late. He has no choice but to keep paddling and hope that he somehow survives the fall.

I take a deep breath and clear my throat.

"Let me put it this way. I like where our relationship is headed. But under the terms of the Rhodes, I can't be married and need to live in college for the first year. I was thinking that if you came to England, we could continue to see each other and, if things work out the way I hope they will, we could get married after the first year."

"So, is that a marriage proposal of sorts?

The canoe tips over the edge of the waterfall, and there is nothing below but mist and roaring water. Fortunately, the waitress comes by and offers to refill our coffee cups. I get a moment to think about what I'm getting into.

This seems like such a big commitment at an awkward time. Until I met Pam, marriage was way off in the future. To the extent that I had given it any thought, I was expecting to focus on grad school and get my career started before even thinking about marriage and family. But the reason I'm about to launch a pre-emptive strike against Pam's other opportunities is because I'm in love with her. Equally important, I'm love with the way she loves me.

Sometimes love can be a very untidy business. It comes calling when you don't expect. It butts in and asks you to make a choice, rearrange your plans, even sacrifice something of your personal freedom and goals in order to gain something better, something that has the promise of fulfilling you in ways that you can't do on your own.

'Okay, Mr. Philosopher,' I tell myself. 'Here's one of those existential moments you always talk about. Real freedom involves making choices and commitments. What are you going to choose?'

I bail out of the canoe.

"Pam, I want you to marry me. I just can't get married now and you will have to trust me. I want you to come with me to Oxford, because I know it will be a time or change and growth for me, and I want us to go through it together. You need to understand, though, that I can't support you and Heather, so you will be somewhat on your own. I will be living in college and you and Heather will need to find a place of your own. Not a great proposal, but it's all I got."

Pam is quiet, thinking.

"You sure you want to do this? You're off on a great adventure with a great future. You'll have lots of English girls hanging all over you."

"I'm not interested. I've never had a relationship like ours, and I want it to continue. And I don't want to run the risk of losing you by leaving you here in the States."

Pam is quiet again.

"I think you need to be sure that you want it. I think it sounds like fun. I probably have enough savings to cover the first few months, but I'll need to find a job. And if I can't find a job, then Heather and I will just come back to the US."

"Is that a yes?"

Pam and I look at each other for a long moment, smiling.

"I would love to marry you."

I float back to the surface of the water, still alive and very much in love. Vienna was a time of enormous personal growth for me, a truly life-changing experience. I expect that Oxford will be also. And something tells me that Pam will be the perfect person to share it with.

In three months, my life has gone from a gentle meander to high gear. If I were a religious person, this would be the time to get on my knees and thank God for rescuing me from my failures, giving me a fantastic second chance and delivering a fabulous wife and companion to my doorstep.

But since I'm not, I just think how lucky I am. The stars lined up, as they say, and Pam and I are off on a great adventure together.

Yeah, it's complicated. But sometimes you have to take life as it comes and trust that you can deal with whatever happens down the road.

And if all else fails, maybe we can fall back on Granny's prayers.

CHAPTER 23
Finding El Dorado

Late November, Oxford

PAM AND I WENT ON a dinner date last night at the Restaurant Elizabeth, across the street from Christ Church College. The meal was exquisite, each course better than the one before, accompanied by great wines. For a graduate student at Oxford, it was a real splurge and the first since we arrived in Oxford in September.

Our lavish feast was made possible by a successful attempt to apply what I have been learning about macroeconomics. A week ago, I opened the Saturday morning paper to see that Harold Wilson, Prime Minister and alum of my Oxford college, had told Parliament on Friday night that the Labour Government had no intention of devaluing the British Pound.

I pondered this for a moment, read the rest of the financial pages, and decided not to take the chance that Wilson might not be telling the truth and/or not able to keep his word. I trundled off to the local National Westminster branch where I had deposited Pam's and my savings in a so-called 'external account', and promptly withdrew the funds in the form of American Express traveler's checks — denominated in US dollars, of course.

Over the weekend, Wilson devalued the Pound from $2.80 to $2.40, and I exchanged the proceeds from the travelers checks on Monday morning with an overnight gain of 15% in Pounds Sterling.

Which led to our extravagant dinner date at the Elizabeth.

And, I sense, a lifelong wariness about commitments made by politicians.

We heard about the Elizabeth from the associate chaplain at my college, a very charming Episcopal priest from North Carolina by the name of Walter Hooper, who is somehow connected to CS Lewis. Walter described a recent meal at the Elizabeth with such detail and color that Pam and I were determined to go as soon as we had the means and reason to celebrate. My weekend 'short' of the Pound gave us both.

I like Jesus a lot. It's a small college, founded in 1571 by a Welsh nobleman. It's the only Oxford College founded during the reign of Elizabeth I, and a rare contemporary portrait of Elizabeth hangs in the dining hall. Due to its scholarship endowment, Jesus has a lot of Welsh students, which I'm told contributes greatly to the quality of singing in the chapel. In terms of 20th century leaders, apart from Harold Wilson, Jesus also produced Lawrence of Arabia.

As she is cracking the hard surface of the crème bruleé, Pam says, "be sure to tell Walter how much we enjoyed our dinner."

"I think you should tell him. In fact, we should take Walter out for dinner sometime."

Pam finally makes it through the thick layer of caramelized sugar and takes a spoonful of incredibly rich and creamy custard.

"I'm a bit amazed at the people you are meeting in Oxford."

"Walter thinks we would enjoy going to Mary Mags sometime."

"Mary what?"

"St. Mary Magdalen church. It's that church in the triangle opposite where you've been working. Apparently, they do an Anglican version of a High Mass, complete with incense."

"Why does he think we would like it?"

"Well, I told him a bit about my Vienna experiences and one-time interest in things Catholic. Walter is somehow attached to Mary Mags. I think he called it an Anglo-Catholic church."

"Well, maybe we'll have to go sometime."

"Maybe."

Actually, I'm pretty unlikely to set foot in any church in Oxford, other than if it is somehow connected with Pam. Oxford is a dream come true in many ways, one of which is the secular intellectual culture of the place.

Contrary to the impression I got three years ago, the University is well beyond its Christian foundations, an intellectually rigorous, scientific world in which religion simply doesn't fit. Sure, there is the form of religion. Every college has a chapel and they still say grace in Latin before meals. But nobody talks about God or faith or church other than the Marxists and then only in a negative way.

This is the kind of intellectual and academic world that I was looking for when I left Utah. Right now, Oxford looks like the El Dorado in my adventure movie, full of great intellectual riches, unbounded opportunities to consider new ideas, and a culture that is resolutely post-Christian. While Vienna now seems like a bit of a detour on the way to El Dorado, I don't regret the time in Vienna or the exploration of Roman Catholicism. It gave me a new perspective on life and a terrific introduction to traditional European culture and history. But the spiritual twist to my quest in Vienna was already fading a year ago and now seems very distant.

I've been in Oxford since early September. I skipped the boat ride with the rest of my Rhodes class so I could get to Oxford before the fall term began and negotiate my way out of doing 'PPE' in favor of a B.Phil. in Economics.

Pam and Heather flew over at the same time. Pam settled in a flat in north Oxford, and Heather is enrolled in a local school, already learning to read (and pronounce) the King's (or Queen's) English. Pam found a temporary job in a local department store, and for now, it looks like this complicated expedition might just work.

Jumping straight into a post-graduate degree in economics is a challenge, but I think it is a better use of the next two years than another undergraduate degree covering philosophy and politics as well as economics. Sometime in the spring I began to rethink what I wanted to do in life. I was filling out my degree requirements at UW with a course in the economics of anti-trust policy. It was fascinating, and I realized that I was (a) actually somewhat bored with philosophy while (b) relishing the insights that economics gave into 'the way the world works.' The more I thought about it, the less I wanted to spend the time at Oxford doing more philosophy, despite the fact that Oxford is in many ways *the* place to study philosophy.

The head of the economics faculty who agreed to let me sit for a B.Phil. proposed that the economics don at Jesus 'supervise' my course of study. The don turns out to be a very bright Englishman with a PhD from Harvard and a particular interest in economics of developing countries.

Jesus is located in the heart of Oxford, on a street called The Turl that connects Broad Street (aka, the Broad) with High Street (aka the High). Exeter is opposite Jesus (in more ways than one) and Lincoln a bit down the street. I've already heard the joke – several times – about the American tourist who couldn't tell the difference between Lincoln and Jesus.

Much of my life in the college is centered on the Graduate Common Room, or GCR. Few graduate students live in college, so the GCR is the place we gather for coffee after lunch, read the newspaper or just keep up with each other. Jesus is a strong science college, so most of my GCR colleagues are doing research degrees in physics, chemistry or other hard sciences, including a shy but charming guy from Ceylon. Another charming friend is the son of the British ambassador to the UN and already tracking towards a career in the Foreign Service. I've also been invited to join a small dining club within the GCR that includes an American Lutheran minister and a German lawyer.

Oxford is a very international university, especially at the graduate level. My friends include Rhodes Scholars from India, Pakistan, South Africa, Australia, New Zealand, Canada, Rhodesia and a couple of other countries in the British Commonwealth. In addition, there are economics graduate students from Africa, Latin America, Greece, Ireland, Japan and various other parts of the world who also turn up at the Institute of Economics and Statistics library.

The effect of this is to expand my horizons yet again. Vienna taught me about Europe. Here I think I'm learning about the world. I'm reading extensively on the economics of developing countries and considering whether to make this a focus of my work in Oxford.

I'm a bit surprised by the activism of the Left. I expected Oxford to be a conservative sort of place, given its role in educating the children of the upper classes – a place where tradition and traditional values would hold sway. But Marxism is generally alive and well in Oxford, with a cross-town divide between the Institute (generally leftish views) and Nuffield College (solidly neo-classical). I spend much of my time in the Institute's larger and more spacious library and bike across to Nuffield, among other places, for seminars.

What I wasn't prepared for is the anti-Americanism at Oxford. Most of this is connected with the war in Vietnam and leftish anti-capitalist and anti-imperialist critiques of the post-colonial era. This is in stark contrast to my experience in Vienna, where the Austrians credit the Americans for saving them from Russian communism and are openly grateful and very friendly towards Americans.

On top of this, my supervisor turns out to be a Marxist. He is careful not to get particularly political in our meetings, but he's very bright and articulate, skeptical of neo-classical economics and the social and political effects of capitalism. Fortunately or unfortunately, I don't see a lot of him. His main job is tutoring undergraduates and his main interest seems to be demonstrating against the war in Vietnam and arguing for more thoroughgoing socialist policies in Britain. Among other indications of Marxist solidarity with the workers of the world, he wears a Chinese workers cap with a Mao pin in the front.

All in all, however, life in Oxford is unfolding in very nice way. I get to make new friends, study an entirely new field at my own pace, have wonderfully stimulating and challenging conversations on all manner of subjects, and roam through the ancient streets and buildings of one of the oldest universities in the world.

This is, indeed, a very nice place to go to school.

CHAPTER 24

Mary Magdalen and Me

Mid June, Oxford

ONE OF THE ODDITIES OF Oxford is that Mary Magdalen has both a church and a college named after her, but 'Magdalen' is pronounced differently depending on whether you're referring to the college or the church. It's *'Mawd-lyn'* College and St. Mary *Mag-da-len* Church, or 'Mary Mags' for short.

It's early evening, and Pam and I are standing in the vestibule, waiting for the Vicar to show up. We've decided to get married in July and picked Mary Mags as the place we would like to say our vows. Father Hooper – no relation to Walter – is a kind, thoughtful man with the intellectual sharpness that comes with leading a church in the heart of a skeptical university town. Hooper has agreed to marry us, but there is a complication.

The complication is that I have never been baptized, as an Anglican or anything else. Pam is, of course, in good standing as far as the Anglicans are concerned because of her Episcopal background. So tonight we're gathering with Hooper so I can be baptized and we can be married as Anglicans. I'm more than a little uncomfortable with this idea, but it appears to be the price of getting married in the church of our choice.

Parts of Mary Mags date from the end of the 12th century, the baptismal fount from around 1350. The church was expanded and remodeled over the centuries, most extensively in the 1840s as part of the Victorian gothic revival. It has an ancient feel, and the services seem straight out of the Middle Ages except that they're in English rather than Latin. Mary Mags is an Anglo-Catholic congregation, 'smells and bells' as the English say. The service is called a Mass, the priests are in full vestments, with censers, bells, chanted liturgy, processions, lots of sitting, standing and kneeling. You're expected to know all the moves as well as the right pages in the Prayer Book.

On the rare occasions that we have been to Mary Mags, I'm always out of step with the liturgy and very aware of disapproving looks from the serious Anglicans who make up the congregation and dislike Americans who can't tell the Prayer Book from the Hymnal. Their disapproval doesn't particularly bother me. I'm here as a spectator, not a participant. If I happen to find the Creed in the Prayer Book in time to read it – most of the congregation has it memorized – I just read it without affirming it. Think of it as interesting ceremony, but not a statement of faith.

I happen to be studying the University crest on the wall when Hooper comes up behind us.

"The Lord is my light. It's the first line of Psalm 27."

We all shake hands and exchange greetings.

"How are the two of you this evening?" he asks.

"We're fine, thank you. Sorry, I didn't catch what you were saying about the psalms."

"I saw you looking at the University crest. *Dominus Illuminatio Mea.* The University's motto is the first line, or title, of Psalm 27 in the Latin Bible. 'The Lord is my light.'"

Hooper pauses briefly to see if I am interested in following up on his point, and then says,

"So, shall we proceed?"

A knot forms in my stomach. The only reason I'm here is so we can get married in a beautiful setting, appropriate to our life in Oxford. I'm not interested in church membership, regular attendance, donating money, etc. It's the building and the ceremony I care about, not the faith. Can I get through this?

"Absolutely." I'm faking it, but I'm determined to gut this out.

"Here's what we'll do. First of all, I want to talk to the two of you about the sacrament of marriage in the Anglican Church. Then, after David and I have a little chat together, we'll gather round the fount and go through the baptismal liturgy in the Prayer Book. Then I'll pour water over David's head, say some prayers and we'll be done. Does that sound all right?"

No, frankly, it doesn't sound all right. But I nod assent. Pam is being warily supportive. She has a good idea of what I'm going through and doesn't want to tilt me one way or another.

Hooper begins.

"Because you don't reside within the parish bounds, we can't post the banns here. As a result, you'll need to first be married in the Registry Office."

"Sorry, but I don't get the bit about banns and the Registry Office."

Hooper smiles, with just a touch of 'Oh, these Americans' in his expression.

"To post the marriage banns is to notify people within the parish that the two of you intend to wed and to invite anyone who has reason to believe that you should not be married to say so, in advance. In the Anglican Church, and especially here at St. Mary Magdalen, you can't be admitted to the sacrament of marriage without posting banns. Your legal marriage will thus need to be done in the Registry Office – I think you Americans call it being married by a Justice of the Peace. But then we will bless it here in the church. You will still say the vows from the Prayer Book. But technically it's a blessing rather than a marriage."

I look at Pam.

"You OK with that?"

She laughs.

"I married you in my heart a long time ago. All this is just icing on the cake."

I take a deep breath and exhale slowly. "So what is the effect of the marriage service?"

Hooper looks at Pam, then at me, then at the two of us together.

"The blessing of a marriage is intended to bring God's grace to bear in your life together. It's not a guarantee of a trouble free marriage, nor even that it will last forever. Marriage is a commitment to each other to be faithful and supportive, for better or for worse, for richer or for poorer, in sickness and in health, for the rest of your lives. To seek God's blessing on your marriage is to make that commitment before God, in the presence of witnesses, and thus to invite his grace into your common life."

Hooper looks at the two of us, as though searching our faces to see whether this is registering. Pam says nothing. I'm thinking it might be a good idea to stop the process after the visit to the Registry Office. But then I think back to the time I decided to ask Pam to come along to England. I wasn't sure what I was getting in for. But I realize that I was committing to the first step towards marriage. Hooper's little speech is clearly designed to test the degree of that commitment.

Finally, I answer for the two of us.

"I think that's something that we would like to have."

"Good, then. Let's proceed."

I think Hooper's pleased by the answer, or at least satisfied, but it's hard to tell through his British reserve.

"David, I'd like you to join me over in the Confessional to go through a prayer of repentance and purity. Pam, if you would be so kind, stay here for just a moment."

My heart sinks. 'Oh, shit', I say to myself. I was hoping that we could get through the formalities of the baptism without too much probing about the state of my soul. What I don't want is an inquisition about my faith or lack thereof, because it could bring this little 'marriage in the church' project to a screeching halt.

Hooper gestures in the direction of a confessional along the wall. It's an open confessional, carved in the gothic revival style to match the Martyr's Memorial just outside the church. No walls, no doors. The penitent is expected to sit on one side and the confessor on the other. Both are in plain view to anyone else in the church. Thankfully, there are only the three of us. Hooper leads the way, and I follow along, my discomfort growing by the step.

We sit down on opposite sides of a small partition, Hooper says a prayer, then asks me if there is anything I would like to confess.

"No, I don't think so."

Hooper seems a little taken aback by this.

"Let's think for a minute. Are there things that you're sorry you did, things that you regret?"

"No, not really. I can't think of anything. I try to live with integrity, doing what I believe to be the right thing at the time. Honesty to myself and others is really important to me. And right now, I honestly can't thing of anything to confess."

Hooper is quiet, thinking. I recognize that my inability to feel sorry for my life may be jeopardizing our chances of getting married in Mary Mags, but I'm not about to make stuff up.

After a long pause, Hooper says, "Well, let's pray. I'm sure that God will show you in due course."

Hooper prays for my absolution and for God to show me areas in my life for which I need his forgiveness. Then off we go back to the fount, which is located just inside the church.

Hooper lifts the lid of the baptismal fount and hands Pam and me copies of the prayer book. As we start into the prayers, a shabbily dressed man steps into the vestibule. It's dark now, and he's half hidden in shadows. He takes off his cap and holds it with both hands in front of him. Hooper seems impatient with the interruption, however, and I'm guessing the guy is looking for a handout, and Hooper knows this.

"What is it that you want?"

"I was hoping you might be able to help us out with a bit of money for food."

"I can't do it right now. We're in the middle of something. Please stand over there and I'll be with you shortly."

I'm desperately hoping the guy goes away. Getting baptized is embarrassing, and I wish Hooper would escort the guy out and lock the door. I don't need witnesses. The man sinks further into the shadows and quietly watches.

We go through the prayers, Hooper puts a cloth on my shoulders, I lean over the fount, and he pours water three times over my head, lays his hand on my head, says some more prayers and it's done. I survive. The presence of the panhandler in the vestibule makes the experience even more awkward. But at least now I have my hall pass to get married.

But Hooper's not finished.

"David, baptism is an entry point into the Christian faith. It's a sacrament, a means of grace that brings you within God's providence and care. It's a step, but only a step towards that illumination we talked about earlier. I hope you will come and take part in the sacraments as often as you can and that you will proceed to confirmation."

We say our goodbyes, and Pam and I leave Hooper to deal with the man in the shadows.

We walk back to our car, past the Martyrs Memorial, the back gate of Balliol and the front gate of St. John's. Along the way, Pam asks, "How are you feeling?"

"Relieved. A little sheepish. I've just been baptized the way they baptize babies. No big bells and whistles. The bum in the corner took a bit of the edge off it. I'm just glad it's over."

For an instant, a question flashes through my mind: 'So what's the difference between you and the bum?' I quickly brush it aside.

Pam squeezes my hand.

"I'm just happy that we're getting married. It doesn't have to be in a church. But I think Mary Mags will be a memorable place to get married. Baptism seems to be the price of admission. I love you for doing it."

I open the car door for Pam.

"I guess this means I can write *Anglican* on the marriage application."

We drive back to Wolvercote in silence.

I've sort of sidled up to religion not because I have had some great religious conversion or really want to join a church, but out of necessity to accomplish the goal of getting married in the way we want. So far, I think I've avoided becoming a hypocrite. I haven't said anything I don't believe, and have gone through a religious ceremony without having to change what I believe or who I am.

In a way, I suppose that's the way Anglicanism works. It's inclusive, and you participate at the level you are comfortable. No counsels of perfection, no big professional apparatus, no rigorous tests of orthodoxy.

The doors are always open to loyal subjects of the Queen – and certain international visitors – for baptism, marriage and burial. I don't know if this is a particularly great way to run a church, but right now it suits me fine.

So much has changed in the last two years since I left Vienna, indeed since that fateful ride on the Vespa in Rome. It's hard to believe that I once considered becoming a Catholic priest.

Partly, it's because the secular world of Oxford has probably done to me what I imagine it has done to its students for at least the last hundred years – weakened or destroyed their religious commitment and faith. Religion is just not fashionable in Oxford. The only Christian I know in Oxford (at least as a Christian) is Walter Hooper.

Oxford seems far more likely to produce revolutionaries than priests. I'm probably no more likely to become a revolutionary than a priest, but my interest in religious issues is waning, and I feel the leftward pull of the culture around me.

Plus, I have moved away from philosophy to economics, from issues of ultimate purpose and meaning to questions of economic welfare and growth.

But perhaps the most profound influence has been falling in love with Pam.

The search for meaning and purpose – at least for me – was bound up with a search for significance. Do I matter? Does my life matter?

When I was alone in Vienna, I couldn't see anything that made it matter. Nothing mattered, and the nihilist fruit of scientific materialism poisoned whatever inklings of purpose for the universe that might be derived from music, art, friendship and acts of kindness. Life had no intrinsic purpose and simply choosing a purpose was fraught with uncertainty and without any assurance that whether any choice was 'true'.

But Pam's love for me, and my love for her and Heather (however feeble it might be by comparison), have filled part of that inner emptiness that could do no more than resonate with the emptiness of an accidental universe.

Maybe love is the only sense of meaning and purpose that I will ever get. But right now, it's enough.

CHAPTER 25

Prague Winter

Late August, Oxford

"WHAT DO YOU THINK THE Americans are going to do?"

The question appeared to be directed at me, as the sole representative of the United States of America in the room.

I was in the Common Room at the Institute, having a mid-morning coffee. Being August, there weren't as many students in the library as usual, but the discussion this morning was pretty intense, and no one was in a rush to get back to their research.

The day began with a jolt when I turned on the radio and heard the BBC news report that Warsaw Pact forces had rolled into Czechoslovakia overnight. NATO forces are on alert, and Western governments have called for an emergency meeting of the UN Security Council. 'Just what we need,' I think, 'another war.'

The news report immediately brought to mind some Czech university students I met in a beer hall in Prague a couple of years earlier and I won-der what is happening to them. I was surprised at the openness of these students with an American who had ventured past the barbed wire of the border between Czechoslovakia and Austria. Prague was liberalizing.

We had an open discussion of history and politics, and their candor was completely unexpected. I could see that they had a dream of a freer, more hopeful future. The 'Prague Spring' that started early this year seemed like such a positive development, one I could envisage my Prague friends being involved in.

But the 'Prague Spring' has now become the 'Prague Winter', and the 'communism with a human face' promoted by Dubcek has been answered with Russian jackboots and tanks. The news reports are that he has stepped down but his whereabouts are unknown.

"I doubt that they will do anything other than protest as long as the Russians don't cross the German border. The US didn't do anything more in Poland and Hungary in the 1950s. Right now they're just a tad busy in Vietnam, and Eastern Europe was conceded to the Soviet Empire at Yalta. I don't think anyone likes what's happening to the Czechs, but no one is going to start a nuclear war over it."

There are some approving nods and sucking on cigarettes by the other grad students.

Someone asks, "Do you think this will affect what the Americans do in Vietnam?"

"I really can't say. It could affect the Presidential election. I think people want the war to be over, but not in a way that looks like the Russians have won. Nixon may do better because he has stronger 'cold warrior' credentials than Humphrey. And there will be more pressure to end the war in a way that assures a modicum of protection for human rights in the South."

"As if the Americans were doing that now or will do so in the future."

The voice comes from my side, and I turn to see one of my more radical colleagues sitting on the arm of a couch, coffee cup in hand.

"No thinking person believes that the Americans are in Vietnam for any reason other than to keep the world safe for American capitalism. The future for South Vietnam is either a Vietnamese form of communism or a dictatorship that satisfies US interests."

I've been in Oxford long enough to have developed a pretty thick skin. Political debate is often blunt, even insulting, with no holds barred. This 'no thinking person' kind of argument is used when the speaker believes that the audience will agree with him and that his opponent can't answer without being seen to be 'un-thinking'. It works best when used on first year undergraduates who may not see the sophistry in the argument.

And it also works as a way of changing the subject, which is what it's intended to do here. We've suddenly moved from the dastardly acts of the Russians in Prague to American imperialism as the cause of all the world's evils.

I wait to see if anyone else will jump into this impromptu debate. It's not that I'm a big supporter of the Vietnam War. But I'm a strong believer in American exceptionalism and in the idealism that is at least one of the motivations to 'pay any price, bear any burden to assure liberty', as JFK said. Also, the radical habit of asserting the moral equivalency of Russian communism and American democracy really ticks me off.

But to make that argument in this setting is useless. So I resort to another Oxford debating ploy – the infamous double negative.

"*I don't think it would be unreasonable to believe,*" I begin, "that the Americans are in Vietnam for a set of reasons, including keeping the world safe for capitalism. There are lots of things not to like about capitalism. But communism is an aggressive ideology and communists are not shy about enforcing their power out of the barrel of a gun, to paraphrase Chairman Mao. In fact, we can have this little debate here today because the American nuclear shield over Western Europe pretty much guarantees that the Russians are not going to cross the German border."

My response does little to reduce the tension. The room is quiet for a minute, then one of my other colleagues takes the conversation in a different direction.

"I think there's a risk of confusing communism *per se* with Russian totalitarianism. Marx himself didn't think Russia was ready for communism because it was still a feudal society and a working class proletariat had yet to emerge. The Vietnamese have lots of reasons to keep their distance from China and prefer the Russians as their major ally. But one can't necessarily assume that a unified, communist Vietnam would have the same totalitarian and imperialist characteristics as Russia."

I wait for a minute to see where this argument is going, then say quietly, "I guess I have yet to see a non-totalitarian form of communism."

People start to drift out of the Common Room. I can see that this conversation could go on longer than I want, so I make a point of looking at the clock, drain my coffee cup and take my leave.

I head back to my customary spot in the library and try to resume reading about Keynes and the Keynesians. After a few pages, I realize it isn't working. I decide to go for a walk. I head towards the University playing fields. It's the kind of warm, sunny day that makes you glad to be alive. And free.

As chance would have it, the walk turns into a philosophical dialogue. I picture myself walking in Russell Square and bumping into a guy in a long black coat, wild dark hair and a full beard flecked with gray.

'Excuse me, is it *Herr Marx*, *Professor Marx*, *Doktor Marx* or *Herr Professor Doktor Marx?*'

He smiles. 'Just plain *Marx* will do, thank you. Of course, I like to be called *Comrade Marx* on occasion.'

'Okay, Comrade Marx, I have a chicken and egg problem for you.'

Marx fixes me with a glare. 'What do you take me for, my dear fellow, a poultry monger?'

'No, no, nothing so mundane or practical. It's a philosophical question.'

Marx relaxes again. 'Go on.'

'It has to do with the *dictatorship of the proletariat*, that phase of historical development between capitalism and true socialism after which the state withers away and the whole society functions naturally on the basis of *from each according to their ability and to each according to their need.*'

Marx smiles broadly. 'A beautiful vision, don't you agree?'

'Possibly. But my main concern is whether we can ever get there.'

'That's because you have not broken free of your capitalist up-bringing. The forces of history are already carrying us towards international justice based on socialist principles. Right think-ing people everywhere can already see the evils of capitalism and the promise of socialism. The key right now is to continue the struggle against capitalism and its pervasive mindset. What you see going on around you now — the wars of national liberation, the rejection of capitalism among students and workers, and the flourishing of international solidarity against the evils of capitalism – are all evidence of progress towards this better, ideal, world. You need to wake up, smell the coffee, change your thinking and join the struggle for global justice.'

I pause to imagine Russell Square in the sunshine with its Georgian architecture and gardens, a stone's throw from the London financial district. Hmm. It appears that Marx is hanging out right in the heart of global capitalism. I wonder why he chose to do his philosophizing in the comfort of the British Museum.

'The question, my dear Marx, is why the victors in this struggle – assuming they're the socialists – will ever choose to let go of power. Getting to the top is never easy, and only the fittest survive. Once there, they are quite likely to decide to stay and enjoy the fruits of victory. If that happens, a new ruling class will emerge and the dictatorship of the proletariat will never fade away.'

Marx runs his fingers irritably through his beard several times, squinting into the sun. Then he turns to me with fire in his eyes.

'Education, young man, education. You can't see the forces of history because you're trapped in the mindset of private property and capitalistic incentives. But when the younger generation is thoroughly indoctrinated with scientific materialism and its ethical norms, there will be neither incentive nor desire to oppress other people.'

I rock back a bit at the prospect of what would be involved in being re-educated to believe in Marx's ideal world. I take a deep breath and press on.

'So here's my chicken and egg problem, Comrade. Which comes first? The all-wise, all-knowing state that educates the people in the right system of values? Or the altruistic leaders and people who create the benign state and then fade away?'

Marx smiles patronizingly.

'That's where the Communist Party comes in. The party is made up of the enlightened, elite thinkers who can see how the forces of history are working to bring about the workers' paradise. They rule for a season, until the goal of a truly just and self-sustaining society is created and then move on to other pursuits.'

'And if they don't?'

'Why wouldn't they, if they are properly selected in the first place.'

'Well, there's this little problem of human nature. Your scientific materialism says that man is just a highly evolved animal. Could it be that the instinct to possess and oppress is wired into the genes? Suppose that your system of education has to go on for a very long time in order to eradicate these bad genetic traits from the population? What if your party elite becomes corrupt long before this process is complete?'

'Young man, you sound like some benighted Catholic who believes in original sin. Have you spoken to Darwin?'

'Sort of. And I think he agrees with me. It seems to me that you face a paradox, Marx. You can't change human nature in a time frame that will allow the state to fade away before it's leadership becomes corrupt and ceases to have an interest in the brave new world of global socialism.'

Marx stops under a tree and turns towards me. The sunlight filters through the leaves and plays on Marx' wiry hair and beard. He looks over his glasses.

'That can't be true.'

'Sorry, I'm not following you. Why not?'

'Because my whole system of thought would collapse.'

Marx pivots and walks back into the British Museum.

My mind drifts back to my friends in Prague.

Traveling from Vienna to Prague, it was clear that you were going into and out of the largest prison camp in the history of man. The barbed wire, watch towers and mine fields stretch for miles, guarded by heavily armed soldiers and rationalized as a defensive barrier against 'infiltrators and spies'. As a guy from the wide-open spaces of Idaho, I found it incredibly depressing. Freedom is such a precious thing.

However, I think what really puts me off about Marxism is the way that communists insist on controlling people's beliefs and their firm conviction that you can bring about the perfect self-governing, egalitarian, free society through education. Marxists are the ultimate 19th century utopian progressives. Progressives generally believed in the perfectibility of man through education and found the Christian concept of innate depravity to be offensive and wrong. I'm no believer in 'original sin' but consider me a skeptic about the power of education to eliminate the Darwinian tendency of human beings to fight for dominance, unless you mean by 'education' Stalinist purges, gulags and executions of 'wrong thinking' people.

I like the idea behind the First Amendment to the US Constitution: the power of the state should never be available to enforce orthodoxy of thought. And the state itself should have no orthodoxy other than the protection of individual rights. Limited government limits the capacity for one group of human beings to oppress and control the rest.

It's probably no accident that the philosophical roots of Marxism are resolutely atheist, anti-clerical and anti-Christian. At one time, I might have been tempted to agree with Marx. Religious belief seemed to me to be ignorant superstition, morally defective and/or a psychological disorder. But seeing the communists' brutal suppression of non-Marxist beliefs, and the prison camp of Eastern Europe, I'm inclined to think that the communists operate an Inquisition that makes Medieval Catholicism look like a model of liberalism.

Sure, the history of Christianity also includes times of repression and civil wars justified by religious differences. But Christianity contains within itself the means to bring conflict to an end. Christians in conflict are people at war with their own belief system. The central ethical precept is 'love one another' and their message is 'peace toward all men.' Eventually, they have to either ditch their faith or stop their fighting.

The same is not true for Marxism. They have their version of the Golden Rule: from each according to ability, to each according to need. But it's a very utilitarian and dehumanizing kind of altruism that makes the individual expendable for the 'common good' and has to be inculcated by force.

I know, I know, the force is only temporary until the whole population has been properly educated and trained in the ways of Marxist-Leninism, at which time the 'dictatorship of the proletariat' fades away. Unfortunately, the dictatorship of the proletariat seems more likely to be a dictatorship of elite power-grabbers, who have absolutely no interest and lots of incentives to never let go of power.

In a way, I wonder if this is also true of atheists who are not Marxists. I remember thinking a few years ago that Christianity as represented by a dominant church like the Mormons or the Catholics was an obstacle to human progress. It needed to be disproved, dismantled and replaced. But with what I wasn't sure, although I was sure that I and other like-minded people could figure out a new foundation for social and personal ethics.

The Marxists have no doubts about what should replace the Church: it's the Communist Party. And their relentless persecution of Catholics in Eastern Europe is only partly about political control. It also tips us to the fact that atheism itself has totalitarian tendencies. It's an intolerant faith that seeks to crush – or at least silence – other worldviews.

Ironically, as on a Christmas Eve a couple of years ago in Mariazell, I find myself siding with the Catholics and other Christians who are being suppressed in places like Czechoslovakia.

Our beliefs are what make us who we are. And, if we're not free to believe, who are we?

CHAPTER 26

Reprieve and Redirection

Mid November, Oxford

"GOOD MORNING, MR. BOCK. EVERYTHING alright with you today?"

I'm on my way to have lunch with Pam in the Market and have stopped by the Porter's Lodge to pick up some mail. The porter on duty is an affable sort of guy who addresses all the students – even the first year undergraduates – as 'Mister' in keeping with Oxford customs.

"I'm doing very well, Frank. Thank you for asking. Temperature's a bit cold, but at least the sun is shining."

"Indeed it is, sir, and we should all be glad of it."

I take the mail out of my box and head for the GCR. I make myself a cup of coffee, throw a sixpence in the kitty and sit down to see what's in the mail.

I'm hoping for a letter from Pam's uncle Jay, who is an Army Colonel currently stationed in the Pentagon. Jay is one of the original Green Berets and has done several tours in Vietnam during the counter-insurgency phase of the conflict. Jay is also an economist who taught at West Point. I've written to Jay for advice about enlisting in the Army.

In September, I got a notice from the Bonneville County draft board that they had classified me 1-A. I had hoped that they would continue my student deferment, but the rules have tightened, and I realize that the next letter I get from them is likely to be a draft notice. Given the US military's appreciation of Rhodes Scholars, I am trying to see if I can negotiate a deal under which I would enlist in the Army, go through OCS in the summer and then get posted back to Oxford to finish my degree. Hence my letter to Jay.

I flip through the mail. There's a letter from Dad and an envelope from the Selective Service Commission of Bonneville County. It looks like the draft process is moving pretty quickly. I really need to hear from Colonel Jay. I open the Commission's letter, expecting to see a draft notice. To my amazement, it's a notice of reclassification from 1-A to 2-S. My student deferment is back in place. How the hell did that happen?

I decide to have a quick read through my Dad's letter before going off to lunch with Pam. I expect she will be pretty happy about the deferment.

I open Dad's letter. The first part is general catch-up. But then I come to a paragraph that explains the Draft Board's decision.

"I know you didn't want me to find out about the change in your draft status in case it might worry me, but Carl told me what was going on. I decided to find out a little bit about how the draft board worked and discovered that the chairman is an old friend of mine."

The wheels begin to turn. Dad's 'old friends' are mostly people whose farms he helped save in the Depression by not repossessing their tractors. Dad was a finance guy for International Harvester and did everything he could to keep from putting his customers into bankruptcy. After the War, when he came back to Idaho as an International Harvester dealer, he had an incredibly loyal customer base.

"So I called him up and asked him about you. He said the change in status to 1-A was a mistake and he would take care of it. He said they are having no trouble meeting their draft quota, and that he and the rest of the board are proud of the fact that an Idaho boy is studying at Oxford. I didn't mean to meddle, but apparently it was a mistake and my asking the question cleared it up."

I take a deep breath, then notice by the clock on the wall that I am late for my date with Pam. I jump up and run next door to the Market. Pam is waiting for me outside *George's in the Market*, a restaurant we frequent because a three-course lunch is ultra cheep in dollar terms.

"Sorry I'm late. I stopped to pick up a letter you might be interested in." I hand her the Draft Board notice. A worried look crosses Pam's face as she studies the form, then she suddenly brightens up.

"They've made you 2-S again! Does this mean you're deferred until you finish Oxford?"

"I think so, although it's a year to year thing. Let's get some lunch, and I'll tell you what happened."

George's is a busy place, and Pam grabs a table while I go through the line to get our lunch. Despite my success in currency speculation, we're both still on tight budgets, and Pam I usually split George's three courses.

I take Pam through Dad's letter. Pam smiles. "Another example of why it pays to have friends."

"Yeah, but it's not necessarily the way I would have wanted it to happen. There is still the possibility that the Draft Board is doing me – or Dad – a favor. Don't get me wrong. I'm not interested in becoming canon fodder in Vietnam. But I also don't want to be seen as a guy who hid out in Oxford while his country was at war."

"So, what are your options?" Pam looks a little tense, but maintains an upbeat attitude.

"I'm wondering if I should pursue the original plan with your Uncle Jay, you know, enlisting, doing OCS and then coming back to finish my degree."

Pam is quiet for a minute. "Honey, the only difference I see in the two options is that it would be the Army that is allowing you to stay in Oxford rather than the Draft Board. And probably for the same reason – that you're a Rhodes Scholar and someone who can make a better contribution to the country by staying in school. At least for now. You can always enlist after you finish Oxford."

Pam looks at her watch. "Oops, I need to get back to work." We walk out of the Market together and say goodbye. Pam looks me in the eyes. "Just know that I'll go wherever you decide to go." She gives me a lingering kiss on the lips, smiles, then turns around and walks off down Market Street. I watch the swing of her hips beneath the new miniskirt and think, 'I am one really lucky guy.'

I decide to take the long way back to the Institute and think about my conversation last fall with the Warden.

The Warden of Rhodes House is the guy who looks after Rhodes Scholars while they're in residence in Oxford. The current Warden – E.T. Williams – was a history don who served as Montgomery's chief of intelligence during World War II. Not much misses his attention when it comes to Rhodes Scholars.

I was invited to tea not long after I arrived in Oxford and met Williams in his study. Williams was affable and friendly, more like a don than a brigadier, but he still had his little rituals of interrogation. I was invited to sit in a chair with an impossibly long seat. If one tried to lean back, you were practically on your back with your feet dangling over the edge. And once you sat up on the edge, it looked like you were nervous. I decided to just lean forward and try to look engaged and engaging.

He asked me general questions about how things were going, which I did my best to answer without getting into trouble. After tea, Williams offered sherry, another endearing Oxford ritual. Following some wonderfully entertaining stories about being in the desert with Montgomery, I asked Williams a very general question about what the Trust expected from the Scholars. Williams tamped down his pipe, took a long puff, and then said in an offhand way: "I always tell people that it's not an investment in a program. It's an investment in a chap."

As I try to process the news about my draft status, I ask myself, 'So, what is this chap going to do?' To be in Oxford is a great privilege, and the sense of privilege is intensified by the fact that my Draft Board has decided to let me stay here.

But I'm not the only one whose Oxford idyll is being disrupted by a war in Southeast Asia. In fact, Vietnam is beginning to slice through our class like a knife. By dint of the selection process, Rhodes Scholars tend to be a patriotic bunch. I think six or seven of the class of thirty-two are military, either academy graduates or ROTC.

But most of us are wrestling with the wisdom of being in Vietnam at all, particularly with main force units fighting a land war in Asia. It's not the sort of thing most would volunteer for, though Marlantes went on active duty as a Marine officer at the beginning of the year and is deployed to Vietnam. Others in the class are taking principled stands against the war, and some against war in general.

And so a new quest begins to take shape.

It's no accident that the conflicts of the Cold War are taking place in poor countries like Vietnam. Communism has had a good innings since World War II, expanding into Central Europe on the back of the Russian Army and taking over China after a century or two of foreign invasions and civil wars. The US is the one country to emerge from World War II in good shape, and the Americans have taken the lead in 'containing' communism and, if possible, rolling it back.

My Oxford Marxist friends would say that the US effort is morally wrong and futile. The 'forces of history' are on the side of communism. I think this is rubbish. But the seductions of Marxism are strongest in the post-colonial Third World. And this is a conflict that can ultimately only be won by broad-based economic growth that knits the world together in a global trading system that is free and fair enough to make it clear that peaceful cooperation and coexistence is preferable to war.

'Now this,' I think, 'is something I can sink my teeth into.' In fact, Oxford may be the perfect place to build the skills and understanding needed for a career in the cause of global poverty reduction, international cooperation and prevention of military conflict.

Is this just hopelessly idealistic? Maybe. But right now it seems like a terrific way for this 'chap' to repay the trust and privilege of being an American Rhodes Scholar at Oxford.

Another scene in the adventure movie comes up on the screen. This time the hero is not in search of gold in the form of meaning, but after a sense of purpose and personal significance. Now the pythons and quicksand seem irrelevant. What's needed is a well-organized expedition. The would-be hero is staring at the high mountain peaks surrounding his base camp and plotting his ascent. The quest is still about changing the culture, about making a difference.

But now it's not religion that is to be conquered and replaced, but war.

CHAPTER 27

Inklings

December, Oxford

IT'S A LATE AFTERNOON IN mid-December and already getting dark. I'm
headed home early to help get dinner ready. Walter Hooper is coming for
dinner with a mystery guest, and Pam won't get home from work until
5:30.

I'm lost in thought about a problem in international trade theory as I
peddle slowly up Banbury Road in the gathering gloom. I come up behind
a double-decker bus that is just pulling out from the Summertown stop,
and I slow to let the bus pull out – better not to contest the right of way
with a big red bus when you're on a bike, I guess.

When my front wheel is about two feet behind the bus, suddenly the
whole back of the bus lights up. It's so unexpected that I nearly lose control of the bike and narrowly avoid crashing onto the sidewalk before real-
izing that the bright light on the back of the bus was the sun momentarily
breaking through the clouds.

The refrain from a favorite Beatles song comes to mind: 'Here comes
the sun… it feels like years since it's been here.' Another challenge of life
in Oxford. Maybe that's why the Brits are so fond of sherry.

Pam and I have developed a settled rhythm to our married life. We're living in north Oxford in a two bedroom flat on the top floor of Summertown House, the University's graduate housing for married students. A year ago, Pam found a job as an accountant for the Officers Club at the US Air Force base in Upper Heyford. By UK standards, it's a good paying job. Not bad for a girl with no prior accounting experience. The base is a half hour drive north of Oxford, but gives us access to the BX, which includes cheap petrol and liquor.

I park my bike in the rack outside the block of flats and head upstairs. Summertown House is full of interesting young families. The Canadian physicist across the hall has twins. The Italian classicist next door is short, older than we are, but married to a younger, stunning girl who is at least 6 inches taller than he is, with a beautiful baby girl. In the evenings, the building fills up with smells of curry.

This Christmas, we have been much more efficient in finding a suitable tree. We put it up yesterday, this time decorated with proper American ornaments and lights from the BX, including thin silver 'icicles'. I'm familiar with icicles, but Pam has an entirely different way of decorating with them.

To her horror, I started to just toss them over the branches.

"No, no, Honey. You can't just toss the icicles like that. You need to hang each one individually so it hangs straight down and makes the tree look pretty."

"You're kidding, right?"

"Not at all. My Dad would always take each one and very carefully position it so the whole tree was equally covered and perfect."

She smiles sweetly, and I start taking off the roughly thrown icicles and meticulously re-hanging them. Naturally, the process seems to take hours. Another lesson in Christmas Pam's way.

I have a list of things to get done before Pam gets home, but it suddenly goes by the way when I walk into the living room. During the day, the Christmas tree has fallen over and is lying in the middle of the room on its side. Worse, all of the icicles are wrapped around the branches and each other, a disaster of major proportions.

I get the tree back upright, clean up the water and begin meticulously untangling the icicles and re-hanging them. Fortunately, I have some practice in this little task from the night before. Pam and Heather arrive home as I'm finishing up, and we all scramble to get dinner ready.

Promptly at 7, Walter arrives with his guest. As always, he's wearing a clerical collar and suit. As he steps into the flat, Walter greets us warmly in his soft North Carolina accent and introduces the mystery guest.

"Pam and David, I'd like you to meet a friend of mine, Priscilla Tolkien."

My wheels are spinning, but I manage to keep calm and give Priscilla a proper greeting and a kiss on the cheek. 'Good gracious!' I think, 'Can she be related to *that* Tolkien?'

Walter and Priscilla step into the living room. They can't miss the Christmas tree, which takes about 20% of the square footage. "My, what a lovely tree," says Priscilla. "It looks like a real American tree," says Walter. Pam beams, I give everyone a crooked smile and keep my mouth shut.

Over dinner, we try to keep the conversation focused on Walter and Priscilla, but they are too gracious and keep turning it back to what we think of Oxford and England. We're not surprised to learn that Walter

and Priscilla know each other because of the longtime relationship between CS Lewis and JRR Tolkien and the others in a group called The
Inklings. We try not to dwell on the two great writers, if for no other
reason to show respect for our guests.

Finally, I ask Priscilla whether her father's books started out as bedtime stories for the children. "No," she says. "The novels were stories on
their own with too many twists and turns and characters to keep track of
at bedtime. But he did tell us other stories that made up."

Pam and I also prod Walter into telling stories about his time with
CS Lewis and about Lewis' robust personality and sense of humor. I nod
along with Walter's description of life with Lewis as if I knew something
about him. In fact, however, I have never read any of Lewis' work and
only know Lewis by reputation, including that many Americans come to
Oxford specifically to visit the place where 'St. Clive' did most of his work.

We sit at the table for a long time, finishing with coffee and some
(barely) drinkable port from the BX. I tell myself it's just another dinner in
Oxford. But somehow there's something special here. It's Christmas, the
tree is up and I'm enjoying the peaceable company of two people whose
lives have been touched by a couple of larger than life Oxford characters.
The only things we're missing are Gandalf and Aslan.

Dinner finishes, Walter and Priscilla take their leave, and Pam and I
turn to the dishes. As we're cleaning up, Pam says, "That was really fun.
Do you think the two of them are dating?" This is a question that hadn't
occurred to me. "Could be," I reply. "If they are, I expect it's something
they keep to themselves."

I hand Pam a plate to dry. "Did you enjoy the evening?"

"Very much. They're both very charming people. How about you?"

"Yeah, I did. Walter is such a great guy. I'm not sure whether he realizes that I'm not a Christian, but it doesn't seem to matter to him. He just assumes I am and keeps sweeping me into his world."

"Is there a problem with that?"

"No, not really. I like having a Christian friend, if only as a counterweight to the secularism and agnosticism of the rest of Oxford. I get worn down sometimes by the passions of the Left. But Walter is also a window into a type of Christian fellowship that is intellectual and gracious."

As I turn out the light in the kitchen, I think, 'Maybe I'll read some of Lewis' stuff some day.'

CHAPTER 28
An Unwanted Reading List

April, Oxford

"HI, HON. WELCOME HOME. I picked up the mail. There's a package for you from someone in North Carolina. It's on the table. Need help with groceries?"

Pam has come just come in from work. She usually shops at the BX before making the drive back to Oxford. Heather, who is a precocious reader, is absorbed in the Chronicles of Narnia but still manages a quick "Hi, mommy" while staying glued to her book.

"No, just a couple of bags tonight. I've got them."

I step into our postage-stamp sized kitchen and give Pam a quick hug and kiss and begin helping unpack the groceries.

"What was in the package?"

"I didn't open it."

Pam steps into the living/dining room and picks it up. "It's addressed to both of us. Open it and see what's in it while I change my clothes."

I sit down at my desk in the living room and tear open the package. In it are four books and a letter from Pam's Aunt Miriam.

Dear Pam and David,

I'm sending you these books about the Holy Spirit because I thought you might enjoy reading them. As you may know, Doug and I have recently come to a new understanding about the Christian faith. Our lives have been changed by the baptism in the Holy Spirit and we want to share it with our family and friends.

We love you.

Blessings,

Miriam

Ah, yes. Aunt Miriam and Uncle Doug. I've heard about them, most recently from Joanna over Christmas during on our visit to Seattle. She said that Miriam and Doug had 'got religion' and were bugging the whole family about it. I also remember a conversation two years ago with Uncle Jay, the Green Beret Colonel recently divorced from Grace, telling me that it was fine to marry into the family, but just make sure I stay as far away from the rest of them as possible. I thought Oxford was safe enough.

Pam starts to fix dinner. "So what was the package about?"

"It's from your Aunt Miriam. She sent some books." There's a small pamphlet called, *The Holy Spirit and You*. There's a book called, *Run, Baby, Run* and another called, *The Cross and the Switchblade*. But the book that really catches my eye is called *They Speak with Other Tongues*.

I look back at the postmark on the package. North Carolina. 'Hmm,' I think. 'And I'll bet they handles snakes, too.'

"Anything interesting?"

I decide to help Pam with dinner. "Can't tell. You should look at them after dinner."

We eat, put Heather to bed, do the dishes and sit down in the living room with the remnants of an inexpensive bottle of Valpolicella from the BX. Pam is reading Miriam's letter and looking at the back cover of *They Speak with Other Tongues*. "It looks like Miriam really did get religion." She sips her wine. "What do you think about the books?"

I take a deep breath. "You want my honest opinion?"

"Sure. At least, I think so."

"I've always been turned off by Bible Belt fundamentalism. It is usually highly judgmental and seriously anti-intellectual. And it has too many similarities to the Mormonism I grew up with. On top of that, fundamentalists are the biggest supporters of the war, have a long and deep history of racism, and are the most vocal supporters of Israel apart from the Jews themselves.

"I can deal with religion in small doses. I like Walter's approach – intellectual, soft-spoken, friendly, inclusive and non-dogmatic. I am not likely to qualify under anyone's definition of a Christian believer. At best, I might be a fellow traveler who comes to the occasional cocktail party. But that's as far as I'm going.

"I don't know your Aunt Miriam. But I'm probably not going to read books about speaking in tongues or whatever else it is that she does. This just isn't the sort of stuff that mainstream Anglicans or Catholics do. Not to be offensive about it, but I would just as soon the books were not in the flat, just in case Heather picks one up."

Pam looks a trifle stunned by my tirade. I'm a little stunned by my tirade. I sound more like the old evangelical atheist David rather than the mellowed religion-may-have-a-place-in-some-people's-lives David.

"That's fine with me," says Pam. "I'll just throw them away." She carries them out to the kitchen and drops them in the trash. "I'm going to bed. You coming?"

"In a minute. I need to do a little work on my thesis."

I sit at my desk reflecting on the emotion generated by Miriam's little gift. I guess I haven't been in contact with the pushy, fundamentalist, anti-intellectual sort of Christians since I left Idaho. I had my fling with Real Thing Christianity in Austria and turned it down. Why would I ever pick up something so down market as 'speaking in tongues'?

In the intellectual refining process of Oxford, I have come to think of myself as a liberal-minded, highly tolerant sort of guy. But there's tolerance and then there's tolerance. Religion is all right as long as it is practiced privately and in a rational way.

We had a local example of the wrong way to do it with a little Sunday School across the road from Summertown House. The couple running it in their home was apparently concerned about the children of we heathen grad students. Heather went for a few weeks, but one Sunday came home talking about the devil. We stopped her from going again, and I had a blunt conversation with the woman running the school. Talk about God is ok, the devil is not.

So, I worry about the sort of religious activism that is likely to be represented by a book with a title like *They Speak with Other Tongues,* sent by a neo-Pentecostal in High Point, North Carolina. Scary. And very unsophisticated.

In any event, I'm glad that Pam isn't interested in following up either. That's a marriage stress we don't need.

CHAPTER 29

In Need of an Ego Boost

Early January, JFK Airport

I FINISHED THE BPHIL ON schedule in June and immediately embarked on an Oxford doctorate. I spent the summer and Michaelmas term defining my thesis topic, which is closely related to the work I've already done on the role of technology in economic development. It's good to have the stress of the exam behind me. The hard slog of completing an advanced degree in a new subject in two years has been worth it.

But now a new challenge presents itself: getting a job that will enable me to support my family while doing research relevant to my topic.

My prime employer target is the UN Industrial Development Organization. With some encouragement from the Warden, I concluded that working for the UN would be an appropriate way to answer the question about how 'this chap' is going to make use of the Rhodes Trust's investment. The longer-term shape of my career will come together in due course. But the broad career goals are clear: working to improve international understanding, build bridges between countries, particularly rich and poor, and contribute in some small way to making war less likely.

During the summer, I went to Vienna to interview with a number of people at UNIDO. I combined the interviews with a family vacation and mini-tour of parts of Germany, France and Austria. We brought Dad over from the States and had a terrific time reconnecting with Clarence and Alberta and retracing my years in Vienna with Pam, Heather and Dad.

When I scheduled the trip, I expected to be actively recruited by UNIDO and offered a job in fairly short order. 'After all,' I told myself, 'I'm a Rhodes Scholar with a degree from Oxford'.

The interview process started off with the personnel officer telling me there was nothing worthwhile that I could do for UNIDO and sort of went downhill from there. By the time Pam, Heather and I left for Seattle to spend Christmas with Joanna, UNIDO and I were still going back and forth on role, reporting relationship, salary, grade and other issues.

My idealistic goal of working for the UN was getting buried under a bureaucratic snowstorm.

Today, we're on the way back to England from Seattle. Pam and I had resolved to put UNIDO out of our minds over Christmas, but during the layover in JFK, I recognized that I had to start thinking about what I was going to do. As usual, I do most of my thinking about such things by talking to Pam.

"Right now, the only option is UNIDO with a sort of entry level job. It's not what I had in mind, though it could still provide the basis for research. But I think the pay needs to be better, particularly because of school for Heather."

Pam has never been as enthusiastic about going to Vienna as I have, but she is being loyal and willing to follow me wherever I decide to go.

"You don't sound very enthusiastic about it."

"I think the UN bureaucracy has just worn me down."

I'm leafing through a file of clippings I brought with me relevant to my thesis and happen to notice one about McKinsey & Company's work in Algeria and Tanzania. Suddenly, I get an idea.

"I think I need an ego boost."

"And where are you going to get that?"

"On the phone."

I walk over to a pay phone, put in some quarters and call McKinsey's New York office. I ask for the personnel department, tell the young woman who I am, explain that I'm just passing through New York, and ask if McKinsey would be interested in talking to a Rhodes Scholar with an advanced degree in economics.

"Why yes, of course. We'd be delighted to talk to you here in New York, but the person you should see in London is Brigadier Langstaff."

She gives me Langstaff's phone number and gets my contact details, which she promises to send him.

"Call him early next week. I'm sure he would be delighted to see you."

I walk back to Pam.

"Well?"

"As I expected. McKinsey is keen to see me. I feel better already."

Pam laughs.

"Are you serious about this? I thought McKinsey was part of the international capitalist conspiracy."

The teasing is well meant and well deserved.

"I think it's worth a shot. At least I'll get to figure out what they do and a bit about how they do it."

CHAPTER 30

A Slight Change of Course

Mid-February, London

"I THINK YOU SHOULD KNOCK off the gas station before you take on the bank."

It's late on a Friday afternoon, and I'm sitting in the offices of McKinsey & Company on Jermyn Street in the west end of London. Actually, I'm sitting in the office of a young American partner who has just flown back from Tanzania, where he is supervising an organizational effectiveness study for the State Trading Corporation. It's dark and raining outside, but McKinsey's Georgian offices are warm and inviting.

This is my eighth and hopefully final interview. Arch Edwards is one of two partners involved in Tanzania. He's originally from Tulsa and retains the folksy humor and language of Oklahoma despite being a summa in English at Princeton, followed by several years in the Air Force and an MBA from Harvard. I'm told he's one of the fastest track partners in recent times. He's also known in the office as 'the Red Terror' for his rigorous and frequently last minute editing with a red ink ballpoint pen.

I got to this afternoon on Jermyn Street somewhat by accident.

I called Langstaff's office the week after we got back from the States and was immediately invited to come down to London to meet him. He's tall, slender and ramrod straight with a clipped accent that belies his British Army background. He's also warm, charming and encouraging. If he's the face of McKinsey, I like the place already. It's certainly the polar opposite of UNIDO.

The meeting with Langstaff has been followed by multiple rounds of interviews with associates and partners, a day with a corporate shrink, and now a final interview with Edwards. Along the way, I've been very impressed by the talent and professionalism of McKinsey, and fascinated with the work they do. It's high impact stuff, with complex problems, intense pressure and client interaction that requires strong communication and interpersonal skills.

And instead of the organization men in grey suits that I expected, I have met some really interesting people, including a guy who took a double first at Oxford and looks like someone who could have been in Sgt. Pepper's Lonely Hearts Club Band. It looks like Carnaby Street is encroaching on Saville Row and Jermyn Street.

By the time I get to Edwards, I'm thoroughly sold on McKinsey, but still not sure if it's the right move for me. And Edwards is the first guy I've met who has worked in Tanzania.

He describes what 'the Firm' – McKinsey, not the CIA – is doing in Tanzania, the internal controversy involved ("we have some partners who think McKinsey should not be engaged with a socialist government") and the conditions attached ("we have made clear to the government that we will not be party to anything that involves the exploitation of the Asians"). This is particularly an issue in the nationalization of the distribution system, which in Tanzania is dominated by South Asians who were brought into Africa by the British and are colloquially know as 'the Jews of Africa'.

As Edwards says all this, I think of my close friend Raman, who was the first Rhodes Scholar of Asian descent to come out of Rhodesia (or Africa, for that matter), and I appreciate the sincerity of Edwards' comments and the ethical integrity behind them.

But then Edwards pulls me up short.

"If you join the Firm, we will expect you to spend up to a year working in our overall corporate practice before you go to Tanzania. The Tanzanians can get lots of economists from the World Bank for free. What they look for from us is something different, a focus on management and ways of making government agencies and parastatal companies more efficient and effective."

I think about this for a minute. The reference to freely available economists hits a little too close to home.

"But my training is in economics. Wouldn't that be where I could be most effective?"

Edwards looks at me, cocks his head to one side and makes his 'knock off the gas station' remark. There's a hint of a smile playing around his mouth and a bit of twinkle in his eye.

I smile back. It's a good point, driven home in an engaging and memorable way.

The interview concludes shortly thereafter. Edwards ends by saying he hopes to see me again soon, and I kind of bounce out of the office into the rain and dark. The ego boost is working. I jump on the Tube to Paddington Station. On the train back to Oxford, I begin to think about the McKinsey opportunity in relation to my research and teaching goals.

My B.Phil. thesis on technology transfer was an exploration of the issues associated with economic growth models. Two factor models (labor and capital) explain relatively little, only about 10% of growth in GDP. So there is a lot of research and modeling to be done on the 'residual factor', and that is where my D.Phil. work is focused. The residual factor includes things like education, knowledge (i.e., technology) and 'know-how' (i.e., how to use resources efficiently and effectively to increase labor and capital productivity and incomes).

It strikes me that McKinsey's potential contribution to economic growth is in improving 'know-how' in both private companies and in government agencies. More importantly, what they do is at the heart of differences in productivity and incomes between advanced and developing economies. Thus, the most important technology to be transferred may not be embedded in capital equipment but in management capabilities.

Suddenly, a whole new quest opens up in front of me – improving the way developing countries are managed. In terms of post-colonial Africa, many if not most development economists cast the government in the 'leading role' as the executive management of the economy. Unless the government has the right skills in planning and execution, the whole economy will struggle and underperform. And that's precisely where McKinsey sits in Tanzania as the advisor to the government on institutional capacity building.

Bingo! This would be a very different approach to the issue of the residual factor in economic growth. It could make a very interesting thesis and research/teaching focus. Experience in McKinsey could be a great foundation. And, I might not be 'just another economist.'

Pam is waiting for me at the station. "So, what did you think?"

On the drive back to Summertown House, I take her though my conversation with Edwards and thoughts about how I could do some interesting research and writing on economics of development.

"Besides, I really like the people I've met in McKinsey. They're practical, can-do people with interesting backgrounds and ambitions. Arch Edwards is very smart, straightforward and a real family guy."

Pam perks up. I know she is concerned about leaving the idyllic setting of our first couple of years together.

"How do you know that?"

"He has pictures of his wife and kids on his credenza. And he talked about how he manages his work and home life. I gather he and his wife have a lot of fun together. Plus, he told me that McKinsey expects men to get the balance right. He said that a divorce would not necessarily kill your chances of making partner, but it could certainly damage them."

"Interesting. When do you hear from them next?"

"As soon as next week. How do you feel about moving to London?"

"Are you kidding? When do we go?"

CHAPTER 31

A Little Miracle of Our Own

May, London

THE LAST YEAR HAS SIMPLY flown by. So many things have happened in our lives. Easily the biggest for me happened today.

The move to London a year ago was a little rocky. We ended up living in a residential hotel while waiting to get into our new house in Dulwich, in order to get Heather settled into a terrific girl's school with the very Victorian motto 'Knowledge is a Fountain Unsealed'. Then, we decided to add to the family. We tried moving to Paris last fall in connection with a lengthy project for a French multinational, but Pam had some issues with the pregnancy and came back to London. I commuted from London to Paris until a month ago when I started a new study for a British shipping company.

As expected, McKinsey started me off in their corporate practice. My first study was to analyze a UK acquisition target for the French multinational. I then moved on to finding acquisition targets for a Dutch company in the UK, France and Germany. After that I went back to France and am now helping figure out how to save the shipping company from a corporate raider. It seems like everything I do these days is associated with increasing international capitalist concentration. So, instead of redeeming Africa from the imperialism of Cecil Rhodes and his friends, I'm doing the sort of thing that Cecil himself would have done.

I guess it would be hard for the Rhodes Trustees to complain too much. Besides, the work is interesting and highly challenging. I have had to come up the learning curve on corporate finance, strategy, and accounting, including building a financial projections model based on France's new consolidation accounting rules – an assignment that nearly killed me, given my zero base in business French, accounting and computer programming. But the client was happy, so my partners were happy, and I get to go off to Tanzania in the fall.

Pam's doctor is the senior gynecologist at Kings College, and in the world of British medicine, he's actually addressed as 'Mister' rather than 'Doctor'. Go figure. As a 'consultant', he's allowed use part of his time and a very good National Health Service Hospital to treat private patients.

Pam is full term in her pregnancy, and this morning she checked into the private obstetric suite at King's College Hospital to be induced. Shortly after admission, her doctor took me aside to make sure that I understood the rules of engagement in the delivery room. I can tell he's not entirely pleased by the fact that I want to be present at the birth. It's just not done in England.

"I should caution you that we will be a very small team in there, and we will be focusing on your wife and the baby. If you faint, we will just leave you on the floor until we're finished with the delivery. Are you all right with that?"

"I don't plan on fainting. But I agree that Pam and the baby should be the priority."

"That's good, then. We'll get started shortly."

The doctor is right to be concerned. I'm not at all sure how I will cope with the sight of blood. Childbirth is an entirely new experience. I really don't know what to expect, and it is quite possible that I will end up on the floor. Although I went along with Pam to a Lamaze course on how to be supportive during labor, that's not the same as being there when the baby is born. Fortunately, Pam has elected to have an epidural, and the breathing stuff may not be all that necessary.

As the anesthesiologist says, "If men had been having babies, we would have invented epidurals a long time ago."

Towards evening, Pam is fully dilated and the crew of three – gynecologist, nurse and anesthesiologist – wheel her into the delivery room. I get a gown, a mask and a spot to stand where I can hold Pam's hand and be out of the way.

After eight hours of labor, everything seems to suddenly accelerate and move at a very fast pace. The baby starts to crown, the doctor inserts the forceps and then all of a sudden, the most beautiful baby girl appears. There's something surreal about it, as though time suddenly accelerates and slows down simultaneously to allow me to take it all in.

I just stand there, speechless, stunned actually, as I watch the doctor and the nurse deal with Pam and the baby. Finally, I blurt out, "Honey, it's a girl."

Pam, of course, can already see all of this in a mirror. The doctor cuts the cord, hands the baby to the nurse who cleans her up, swaddles her and puts her in a clear plastic cot on wheels. The doctor congratulates me and suggests that now would be a good time for me to retreat to the waiting room.

It takes some a little while for things to finish up in the delivery suite, and I have time to reflect on what just happened. Pam and I went into the delivery room as a couple. And now there is this incredibly beautiful little girl. The thought keeps running through my head, 'I have just seen a miracle… I have just seen a miracle.'

Pam and the baby eventually get wheeled back to a private room. The team moves her into the bed, the nurse tucks her in, and we are left alone with the baby.

"How are you doing?"

"I'm tired and the epidural is wearing off. What do you think of your baby girl?"

I lean over the cot and look at the baby. She's swaddled tightly but one hand and her head are out. I can now see the reddish blond hair.

"I think she's perfect. Ears, mouth, nose. I'm amazed at how pretty her hands and fingers are, complete with finger nails."

"It's amazing, isn't it?"

Pam has been through this before, and she's very tired, but she still manages to be as enthusiastic about the baby as if it were her first.

I sit on the edge of Pam's bed and hold her hand.

"Looks like we have an Angela."

"Are you disappointed that it wasn't a boy?"

"Are you kidding? This is love at first sight."

Later, Pam settles in for the night, and I head home. It's a warm sunny evening in London. The birds are singing, all is well with the world. I keep thinking about what an amazing day it has been. It started early with the check-in at the hospital and ended in a staggering experience of life and love. I simply was not prepared for the emotional impact of watching my daughter be born. I can't imagine not being there. What *are* all those British husbands thinking?

Our townhouse is in a new development on the Alleyn College Estates. It's part of a group of townhouses built around a small wooded area. The ground floor is fitted out as a study and au pair suite, the main living area is on the second floor with floor to ceiling windows front and back, and the bedrooms are on the third. We found the house through a McKinsey associate who lives two doors down. Richard and Sally have since become wonderful friends and have been taking care of Heather for the day.

I stop by to pick up Heather, delivering the news that she has a new baby sister. She's excited, but also a little apprehensive. After all, she's been an only child for 8 years. We walk the two doors down to our house, go up to the living room and call some family and friends in the States to let them know the happy news.

I'm really touched by the reaction of my friend Selwyn, another McKinsey consultant. Selwyn is a marketing guy who speaks multiple languages (including Serbo-Croatian), sings in the London Bach Chorale, and has a circle of interesting artistic friends, including an up and coming lithographer whose work is starting to decorate our house. Selwyn jumps in his car and drives over from Clapham Common with a bottle of champagne, 'to wet the bay's head' as they say in England.

A makeshift party develops in our living room. Selwyn pops the cork on a bottle of Veuve Cliquot, and we all drink a toast to Pam and the baby.

"And, here's to you, old man." Selwyn raises his glass and the others join in. "How do you feel?"

Selwyn's father worked for the Bank of England but was killed in World War II when Selwyn was a small child, and he grew up in a single parent household. He has recently had his first child and knows the poignancy of becoming a father for the first time.

I've long since adopted Heather and already know a lot about the father-daughter relationship. Fatherhood is somewhat old hat by now. But witnessing a birth is entirely new.

I take a sip of champagne.

"Gobsmacked. I wasn't sure what to expect in the delivery room, and Pam's doctor didn't help by telling me that if I fainted they would just leave me on the floor. You know, you get excited at the beginning of the pregnancy, then get used to it, and then it culminates so suddenly. When the baby came out, I was just stunned by the fact that here was a new life, a new human being."

I drink some more champagne.

"I would have to say that I have witnessed a miracle. Literally."

Everyone is quiet for a moment. Then Selwyn asks, "What have you decided to call her?"

"Angela. Angela Beth."

Selwyn smiles. "A little messenger of the Lord."

"Sorry, I'm missing you."

"Angela means messenger, angel of God. Your miracle baby is a message all by herself."

"Yeah, I can see how that might be true."

After everyone leaves, I sit in the darkness of the living room, thinking about the events of the day. I know the phrase, 'I've seen a miracle' is more than just an expression. I think back to the professor in Vienna: '*Es ist ein Wunder.*' Something more than just a remarkable event, a passing fancy. This was real, transcendent, an experience that cannot be encapsulated in a purely materialistic description of reality.

As I think further, it's not the birth itself that is miraculous. It's the meaning that it has for me. I'm a father in a different sense than I was when the day began. And I have experienced the instantaneous love that happens when parents see a new child for the first time.

Yeah, yeah, I know, some will say it's just biology, the instinct for survival and reproduction expressing itself and being (mis)interpreted by my brain as an emotion called love. I remember thinking and saying similar things several years ago in the height of my hardline atheism. My former views now look incredibly shallow and simplistic.

The real truth is that a human mind is – or at least mine was – viciously capable of stripping everything of meaning. You simply *choose* a cynical interpretation of profound experiences when the first reaction or 'intuition' with respect to ordinary things like a baby's ear or finger may be awe, wonder, joy and/or love.

Maybe there's a deeper truth in what we call love. Maybe it's not just the experience of having another person affirm *us*, but that we have within us the capacity to love one who can't (yet, at least) love us back. Maybe, just maybe, we really find our meaning and significance as human beings not so much in being loved but in the act of loving someone else (or several someone elses).

Lots to think about. But my little 'messenger of God' has already taught me something very profound. One thing is clear: life will never be the same.

CHAPTER 32

A Muddy Jesus

August, High Point

"How are you enjoying the reunion, David?"

I've just run into Pam's Aunt Miriam in the driveway of her home in High Point, North Carolina. Miriam is hosting a family reunion for her four sisters and their children. Pam and I flew into New York from London, spent a few days with Joanna at her new home in Connecticut, and then drove down to North Carolina. It's my first trip south of the Mason-Dixon Line.

"I'm having a good time, Miriam. It's fun to meet Pam's family. I grew up in a small family with few relatives, and I've never been to anything quite like this before."

Miriam gives me a knowing sort of smile.

Besides the four sisters, there are about 15 cousins, of whom two are married – Pam and Miriam's oldest son, Stewart. Our two girls are the only grandchildren. Miriam's husband Doug is away on business. Uncle King decided to pass on the opportunity to get together with his four sisters and their families.

On the drive down with Joanna and one of Miriam's sons, I've learned a bit about Miriam and Doug. They recently moved to High Point after he retired from the Air Force. They were given use of a 20-acre estate with a lake, a main house and two cottages as a center for their work with college age boys and girls. Doug was in counterintelligence for much of his Air Force career, but his last assignment brought him to eastern North Carolina to oversee the ROTC program at East Carolina U. Miriam is a linguist who translated Russian scientific articles while raising five boys.

"And what do you think of your wife's extended family?"

Miriam has blond hair, clear blue eyes and the same large smile as Joanna. But I recognize that this isn't an idle question.

"Very interesting group. I'm just getting to know some of them."

I decide to change the subject before I get too deeply into family politics. I know too much already, including the fact that the rest of the sisters are not happy that Miriam and Doug have 'got religion'. The sisters fled anything to do with their mother's evangelistic activity and have lived without any religious life or with very conventional ones. Miriam's conversion sent minor shock waves around the family. It's also the elephant in the room at the reunion.

"You're amazing to host this reunion. Such a lot of work. I've heard a bit about what you do here. What made you and Doug decide to move to High Point?"

Miriam smiles.

"We lived in Greenville for the last few years of Doug's career in the Air Force. Doug and I always went to church but we were not very serious about our faith. One day someone invited us both to a meeting where we heard testimonies about being baptized in the Holy Spirit. We never imagined being a Christian could be exciting but these people were very excited about what the Lord was doing in their lives. We decided to pursue it ourselves. It changed our lives, and God started to do remarkable things at ECU.

"As Doug was retiring, he told friends that he would like to continue working with young people. A woman here in High Point owned this property, which was not being used. She offered it to us and asked us to use it as a place for ministry. Doug and the boys who usually stay on the estate have cleared it all out and restored it. It had become very overgrown."

Miriam looks off across the lake, and I follow her gaze. A well-maintained lawn runs down to the lake, which is rimmed with azaleas and rhododendrons. The mature oaks and hickories give shade from the August sun. Several of the sisters are sitting in the screened gazebo next to the pool. The cousins are scattered around, some playing tennis, others swimming or sunbathing.

"So what do you do here?"

"We invite young men and women, mostly college age people, to live here for a season while they get established in a Christian life. Many come from difficult backgrounds and need healing and deliverance as well as teaching and mentoring. Doug works with the young men and I work with the girls. We also teach small groups that meet in various homes. Doug is making a circuit this week but will be back tomorrow."

"So what happens to people who come here?"

Miriam is an interesting person, and I'm enjoying the conversation. I realize that I'm asking too many questions and getting in deeper than I should. The one thing I don't want is to become a target for her evangelistic pitch.

"One of my favorite stories is a young man who was on drugs and living on the street. His parents asked if we would take him in. We prayed with him to accept Jesus as his savior and to be baptized in the Spirit. He was set free from all manner of evil spirits and healed of his drug addiction. One day he was helping clean out a spring that was full of leaves and mud and muck. He was down in a hole clearing the muck out with his bare hands when the spring started to flow again. He looked up at me all covered with mud and said, 'Look, Mrs. Carty. This is what Jesus has done for me. He's made the clean water flow in my life. He's washing out all of the muck.'"

Miriam smiles the big family smile. I can tell she's watching to see how I might be reacting.

I maintain a poker face, but the story catches me by surprise, and for a moment, I feel deeply moved by the picture of a young drug addict finding hope. I wasn't expecting anything so dramatic, and Miriam tells it in a calm, matter of fact way, which only heightens its impact. The stuff about evil spirits seems quaint and weird, but I can see that Miriam is very sincere and genuinely believes that somehow Jesus had something to do with the addict's cure. I hear a distant echo of another time when I encountered people in Austria with a similar sense of purpose, rooted in their religious beliefs. I feel admiration and a touch of envy for them, even if I don't understand why they do it or why it works for them.

But it's time to move on.

"I get the sense that some of your sisters are not too happy about your new religious experience."

Miriam laughs.

"We were very competitive growing up. We used to compete over everything, especially boy friends. Our mother was an evangelist and away a lot. None of us really wanted to be like her. The younger sisters were pretty rebellious. Typical preacher's kids, I guess. I think they're afraid that we'll become narrow and legalistic like our mother and her friends. You know, no drinking, no dancing, stuffy, boring and no fun to be with."

I look over at Miriam's sisters in the gazebo. Two are smoking cigarettes and still a little hung over from last night. All three are good-looking women but two are divorced with troubled kids, dark circles under their eyes and blotchy complexions. Uncle Richard says jokingly the only reason they keep him around is because they need someone to carve the turkey at Thanksgiving. Miriam, on the other hand, looks younger than her age, has lovely skin and a glow about her.

"So, how do you handle that?"

"Mostly through prayer. After Doug and I were baptized in the Holy Spirit and began to pray in tongues, we discovered that lots of things started to change in our lives and in our friends' lives. Satan has really ravaged our family. But we believe the Lord is working to redeem everything. We also send books."

Miriam smiles and gives me a little wink. Miriam says all of this in her relaxed, natural way — serene would probably be the best description — including the matter of fact way of she alludes to the devil.

"And is it starting to work?"

"It will take some time. Mother prayed for all of us every day of her life. She died without seeing any of her children walking with the Lord. Now Doug and I are, and most of our boys."

A mischievous smile appears on Miriam's face.

"We find that younger people are much more open to the Spirit than our generation is and that parents are often led into a new spiritual experience by their children. So we're just going to pray for all the cousins."

Miriam smiles again. There's a twinkle in her eye.

"And for their husbands."

CHAPTER 33

A Dark Cloud on
a Sunny Day

September, London

TODAY WE CHRISTENED ANGELA AT the local village church.

It seems strange to talk about a village church in the midst of south London, but we actually live close to the village center.

Dulwich has a recorded history going back to the 10th century and Edward Alleyn, a successful Shakespearean actor and entrepreneur, purchased the estate our house sits on from Henry VIII. Alleyn established a school called Alleyn's College of God's Gift and the Alleyn College Estate is our 'landlord' in a peculiarly British way. The Estate still owns the property and we have a 99-year lease on the land and improvements, after which our house, if still standing, will revert to the Estate.

This legal structure doesn't particularly appeal to my Idaho inclination to own property in fee simple form. Here I'm a tenant but in effect paid the builder for the house – aka, 'improvements' – while the Estate has title to it. But it's the way things are done here. I guess the best part about it is it keeps large tracts of land and their improvements under the control of a party that has a long-term interest in preserving the value of the entire development, including for today's purposes the village and its church as well as the toll gate we have to pass through to get to the village.

St. Barnabas is another example of Gothic Revival architecture, and the church is modeled on a 15th century church elsewhere in England.

Once again, form has trumped function. Our purpose is to get Angela baptized. We want it to be in nice surroundings. Plus, it's a sunny day, always an auspicious sign in England.

This is another religious novelty for me, though not for Pam. She was baptized as an Episcopalian, as was Heather. It's the thing you do with babies. I think I've been to only one other christening.

We've squeezed this affair between the family reunion in the States and our imminent departure for Tanzania, where I will be part of the McKinsey team implementing a comprehensive reorganization of the Tanzanian government. We're having a champagne brunch after the christening and then madly packing to leave for Dar Es Salaam.

This is the second time we've been in St. Barnabas, the first being our scouting expedition to see if we liked the setting. There's another couple getting their baby baptized, and they look about as familiar with St. Barnabas as we are. Sally and Richard have agreed to be godparents, even though they are wary of organized religion themselves.

The Vicar directs us to the fount, which is located at the base of the church tower. He identifies the parents and godparents, distributes copies of the Book of Common Prayer and gives us an overview of what is involved. We all nod assent. Unlike my own baptism a few years ago, this time I decide to pay attention to the words of the service.

After all, this is my baby girl, and I want the whole experience to be memorable.

The Vicar starts reading from the Prayer Book service:

"Dearly beloved, forasmuch as our Saviour Christ saith, None can enter into the Kingdom of God, except he be regenerate and born anew of Water and of the Holy Ghost; I beseech you to call upon God the Father, through our Lord Jesus Christ, that of his bounteous mercy he will grant to this Child that which by nature she cannot have; that she may be baptized with Water and the Holy Ghost, and received into Christ's holy Church, and be made a living member of the same."

For a moment, I feel like interrupting the Vicar. The language is wonderful, but I suddenly have an urge to ask questions. What do you mean by 'Grant what she cannot by nature have...' Or, 'be baptized with water *and* the Holy Ghost?' Alas, this is not the right time to get theological, so I let it pass and try to focus on the service.

Angela is in Pam's arms, kicking her legs, seems to be taking it all in – appropriately for a 5 month old – and jabbering from time to time, but easily quieted.

Then we all read together, inter alia: "Give thy Holy Spirit to this Child, That she may be born again, And be made an heir of everlasting salvation..."

'Whoa! Hold on a minute,' I think. 'What's this about being *born again*? As an Anglican? I thought that was for fundamentalists. Did I do/say that when I got baptized? Can I get a do-over?'

The Vicar reads some more prayers, then turns to Sally and Richard and asks them to respond on behalf of Angela.

Most of the questions are straightforward but I suddenly get hung up again on one in particular:

"Dost thou, in the name of the Child, renounce the devil and all his works…?"

A dark cloud seems to pass over as the Vicar says this. My feathers are ruffled, much as they were with the incident with Heather and her erstwhile Sunday school. If it weren't for the fact that this is couched in antiquated language, I might actually object to mention of the devil in connection with my amazingly beautiful and perfect baby girl. I decide to let it pass.

After yet more prayers, the Vicar takes Angela in his arms, dips water over her head three times, prays for her, and hands her back to me. She blinks a bit from the water, but is performing the role of the baby perfectly. The Vicar takes up a collection and we are done.

We walk out into the English sunshine.

I have a wonderfully happy feeling about being able to experience and give to my family something that I never had myself. The Elizabethan language of the Prayer Book is mesmerizing. I see why people do these things even though they may not totally believe the words. I guess this is what I like about the Anglican Church. A rich heritage to which you can gain access by virtue of being a loyal subject of the Queen – as in the case of Angela – or simply residing in the right places – as in my case.

I can't help drawing the contrast between Catholics and Anglicans.

Catholics put a lot of emphasis on proper qualifications. Not just anyone can participate in the Eucharist. And there are significant hurdles to get to baptism. You have to qualify to take part in the Catholic sacraments. The Anglicans, on the other hand, seem to reverse the process. Make it easy to access the sacraments and trust somehow that God will sort things out later.

For a guy who, if asked, would say that he's not a Christian, I like the Anglican way better.

At the end of the day, my mind drifts back to certain words in the Prayer Book that particularly caught my attention, including especially the mention of the devil.

I simply don't understand why one would preserve concepts and language that refer to a personal devil. This is such a medieval idea, long since discredited and banished from intellectual life. To keep it in the Prayer Book is to blindly hold to tradition in a way that actually presents a barrier to educated people ever embracing the Christian faith.

Unless, as I suspect, most Anglicans just hold to the historic Prayer Book out of respect for the tradition, even if the tradition is untrue, because the Anglican tradition itself serves such an important role in defining and maintaining what it means to be English. In this sense, the Prayer Book is a vital connection between the present and the past, so revising it to make it modern would defeat its social purpose. You don't have to believe it, just accept it. Or something like that.

Despite having been baptized in an Anglican church, I'm still very much the American rationalist. The concept of a personal devil is outdated and best not mentioned in polite company. And I don't see the utility of giving him space in a baby's baptism service.

The dark cloud lifts a bit but still lingers as I go to bed. It was a wonderful day in any event.

CHAPTER 34

Train Wreck in Tanga

December, Northern Tanzania

"THERE'S A TRAIN COMING."

I'm in the back seat of a government Land Rover driving back to Tanga from a visit to two different *ujamaa* villages in northeast Tanzania. My traveling companions – two government officials and the driver – are engaged in an animated conversation in Swahili. The driver is half-turned towards the back seat and glancing back at the road from time to time. Fortunately, there is little or no traffic on the highway, and we're not going all that fast.

But we're approaching a railway crossing, and there's a slow moving steam locomotive and two dozen or so railway cars moving down the track. I see it, but no one else does. I watch it long enough to see that the train and the Land Rover are going to arrive at the crossing at about the same time. Being careful not to startle anyone – particularly the preoccupied driver – I calmly draw attention to the oncoming Iron Horse to our left.

The District Officer in the back seat with me hears me over the Swahili, looks up and suddenly shouts, "Train!" At which point, the occupants in the front seat suddenly turn their attention to what's out front

218

and begin shouting, "Train! Train!" The driver slams on the brakes and the Land Rover skids to a halt just as the East African Railways Express (sort of) rumbles across the road.

There's a sudden burst of appreciation for the non-Swahili speaking management consultant in the back seat whose visit to Tanga triggered this little *safari* into the bush. "It's good you saw it." "We would have all been killed." I breathe a sigh of relief, as the driver starts up, carefully looks both ways and proceeds across the railway line.

A near train wreck is probably an apt metaphor for this trip, as well as for my first few months in Tanzania.

I'm part of the McKinsey team that is advising the Tanzanian Government on a top to bottom reorganization of the national government, from the central ministries in Dar to the District Administrations everywhere in Tanzania. It's a big project, one that has the full support of President Nyerere. The design team rotated back to London and elsewhere during the summer, and now it's down to the heavy lifting of figuring out how to make the concepts work on the ground. In terms of my goals in joining McKinsey, it seems like the perfect project.

Life on the ground, however, is a bit different.

We arrived in Dar in September, got Heather into the International School and settled into our house a couple of miles north of downtown Dar. Fortunately, we inherited a government house and car and five servants from the previous engagement manager. It's a very nice place, set in an acre of mango and papaya trees with bougainvillea spreading over the carport. The only problem was an infestation of cockroaches the size of large mice and some spiders in the mango trees with webs large enough to catch birds. We called the exterminators to blast everything in sight, which included spraying the interior walls with DDT, the only effective way of controlling malaria in the tropics. I feel a twinge of guilt. I know Rachel Carson would not be happy, but we have a four-month-old baby to worry about.

We've also joined the yacht club, bought a small sailboat, and done some snorkeling in the Indian Ocean. Pam and Heather are into horseback rides through the coastal area. We still can't get used to the American-style drive-in movie theater that sells beer and *samosas* in the concession stand. We usually do lunch together around the pool at the Hotel Kilimanjaro.

Today's *safari* outside Tanga is part of some fieldwork to test the organizational model. I asked to see a couple of *ujamaa* villages, which are key to the goals of African socialism as laid out by Nyerere in the Arusha Declaration. Nyerere is a charismatic individual, with a gift for politics and a degree from Edinburgh University along with a good dose of Fabian socialism. He's a practicing Catholic, and from all appearances an honest and humble guy. The government is made up of technocrats who mostly take their jobs seriously and live on their civil servants' pay.

What rocked me today was seeing just how poor and underdeveloped Tanzania is.

I was naively expecting to see thriving villages of several hundred people, complete with school, medical center, marketplace and smiling children – African socialism at work. However, the first village seemed randomly located with a few mud huts and less than a dozen people in sight, most of whom appeared to have nothing to do. The District Officer was a little embarrassed as he explained that most of the people were working out in the fields, none of which were visible from the village or on the drive to it. Progress in the village consisted of a water standpipe, a cement floor to the *go-down* (warehouse) and a coconut tree nursery. Next on the list of planned improvements are some oxen to pull plows, once an ox trainer becomes available to teach the villagers how to care for and use the oxen.

None of these are insignificant. The standpipe saves the women a two hour round trip to get water in a jug on their heads; the cement floor reduces grain loss to mold and vermin; and the tree nursery is leading to a new cash crop for the village. But the connection between what I'm doing with McKinsey and what Tanzania needs is hard to see.

As I leaned over the fence of the coconut tree nursery and listened to the District Officer tell me how to grow a coconut tree, I realized that I had no skills or knowledge that would be remotely useful here, other than some plant and animal husbandry I picked up around the farms of Eastern Idaho. Even that seemed likely to be irrelevant to the Tanzanian situation. The thought kept going through my head, 'I have nothing to contribute here.'

I kept my thoughts to myself and went off to see the next village. Same story, except the village is even less developed. The day has definitely been a train wreck between my expectations and reality in the African bush.

On the way into Tanga, we start talking about a news story of a District Officer being killed by a farmer with a shotgun. I have a hard time relating the story to what I have seen today.

"So, how did the farmer get the shotgun, and why did he shoot the DO?"

There is an uneasy silence in the Land Rover, then the District Officer explains. "He was what we call a 'large farmer', with about a hundred acres of land, with a large number of hired workers living together in a village on his property. The government has decided to convert these large farms into *ujamaa* villages. The DO was responsible for implementing the policy, so the farmer took out his anger on the DO."

"I see," I say. At the same time, I hear the whistle of an approaching train in my mind. So the Tanzanians are doing what socialists do – expropriating capitalists, in this case an African farmer who has been clever enough and hard working enough to create a small estate. And I feel the rumble of another set of expectations being crushed under African – or socialist – realities.

The District Officer drops me off at the Tanga airport for the short flight back to Dar. He's a kind and sincere public servant. I wish there were something more I could do for him, other than explain how the reorganization is supposed to give him more authority and resources. He thanks me, but his eyes tell me he's seen this before. He's had other smart young Europeans and Americans come up to Tanga and tell him how Tanzanian development is really going to take off. He's far too wise to let his hopes be raised by me.

At least the main reason for coming here has been achieved. Moving authority and responsibility down to the District level is clearly the right idea vs. the current system of central ministries holding national budgets and operating in an uncoordinated fashion all the way down to the village. We've got the concept right, now all we have to do is break up the power centers in Dar. Sounds like lots of fun. Where the hell are those guys who made this recommendation?

Pam picks me up at the airport. "So, what's an *ujamaa* village like?"

"A few mud huts and a water pipe. I think they've got a long way to go."

"And?"

"I came away feeling like I have nothing to contribute. They need ox trainers, not management consultants."

That night, I have a hard time going to sleep.

It's not just the realities of an *ujamaa* village. It's also the reluctance of the newly appointed regional and district development officers to take the job. We think we've designed the dream job for a smart, entrepreneurial executive who wants to make a difference. We've consolidated authority and resources, set up planning and control systems and asked the government to pick the best people in the Tanzanian Civil Service, drawn from whatever ministry necessary. We've promised that they will have the budget and support to succeed.

But they really don't want the job, and initially they were not very forthcoming about why. We thought maybe they were insufficiently ambitious. It turned out that they think we're crazy to create positions that are so transparently accountable in the political context of Tanzania. They have had good careers thus far, and they can see that they will get blamed for everything that goes wrong in their region or district. So they're negotiating with us and with the President's office to fuzz things up a bit.

On top of that is the resistance from the mandarins in the central ministries that are the traditional centers of power and budgets. Breaking this down is daunting, as I know personally from several encounters with the head of the health ministry – a physician whose top priority is building a medical school and teaching hospital rather than training lower skill village health workers for the districts.

I hear the *askari* walking around the house. For some reason he insists on walking noisily on the gravel next to the jalousie windows. At least I know he's on the job. A cool breeze and the sound of drums in a nearby village come through the windows.

What's really keeping me awake, however, is a conversation a few days ago with one of my Tanzanian counterparts. He's a rising star and was asked to accompany a high-level delegation on a visit to China. He wandered over to my desk and asked if he could borrow my ruler.

"Uh, Charles, I'm afraid I don't have a ruler."

"Yes, you do. That plastic thing you use to draw charts."

"Oh, the template." Standard issue for all McKinsey associates is an official McKinsey charting tool with cutouts for various rectangles, lines and circles so you can draw organization charts and flow diagrams. I'm reluctant to let it out of my sight.

"Do you mind if I ask why you need it?"

Charles gives me an awkward look. I don't think he wants me to know what he's working on.

"I'm writing up the report on the high-level delegation's visit to China, and I need to explain how the Chinese government is organized."

"How about I help you? I have some experience in these things."

Charles and I sit together around my desk. He goes through his notes and I drive the charting tool. Pretty quickly we have a complete organization chart of the Chinese government, top to bottom, with the parallel Communist Party structure on the side. I sit and look at the finished chart for a moment.

"Charles, does that look familiar to you?"

Charles scrutinizes the chart. "Maybe. What do you mean?"

I reach into my desk drawer and pull out the McKinsey report on the proposed organization structure for Tanzania and lay it out next to

Charles' chart. The two charts are practically identical. Charles laughs. I smile wanly.

I suppose I should be happy. Good organization is good organization whether it's designed by McKinsey & Company or the Chinese Communist Party. But I don't feel that way. I feel like the Alec Guinness character in 'The Bridge on the River Kwai' who realizes that he has deployed his technical knowledge for a purpose entirely contrary to his values and mission.

So what am I doing in Tanzania? Am I really contributing to the Tanzanian economy? Am I helping build a political system that I don't fundamentally agree with? Am I a high paid technocrat? Or someone with a broader purpose?

At this point I remember some advice Arch Edwards, now my McKinsey mentor, once gave me. 'When you start thinking dark thoughts, it's time to drink a glass of warm milk and go to bed.' I trundle off to the kitchen and pour myself a glass of the Danish milk that has to be imported because the government nationalized the local dairies. Nobody said that economic development was easy.

CHAPTER 35

Chinese Fortune Cookies

January, Dar Es Salaam

DRIVING OUT TO THE CENTRAL Motor Pool in Dar, I'm thinking that it's likely to take the whole day to get our government-issued VW Squareback serviced. Things just don't happen all that fast in Tanzania. But I'm still under the weather from a bug I think I caught in Tanga, so I'm probably not that useful in the office anyway.

The Motor Pool is surrounded by a 6-foot chain link fence with a guard at the entrance gate. I drive up to the gate, expecting to have to explain what I'm doing there and why a white guy is driving a government car. To my surprise, the guard waves me through the gate and points to the service area off to my right. 'Wonders never cease', I think.

The service area is a beehive of activity. As soon as I pull up, a mechanic in uniform comes up to the car.

"Are you here for servicing."

"Yes, I am."

"Any problems with the car?"

"No, just needs an oil change and lube."

"Okay, please step out, and I'll take it from here."

The mechanic jumps in the car, pulls it into the bay and two or three other mechanics begin immediately working on the car. I haven't seen anything like it since I left Idaho. I'm still standing in the driveway when I hear a British accent behind me.

"So what brings you to Tanzania?"

I turn around to see a very Chinese-looking man coming towards me. He's slender, shorter than me, with short gray hair and a loose fitting shirt. He introduces himself as Mr. Li, the manager of the Motor Pool.

"I'm a management consultant. We're working on a reorganization of the government."

Li smiles. I can tell he's sizing me up to see if I have any clue what I'm doing in Africa, so I decide to quickly change the subject.

"Do you mind if I ask how you came to be the manager of the Motor Pool."

Li laughs and sticks a cigarette in his mouth. "I'm originally from Singapore." He lights the cigarette and talks a long draw. "I tangled politically with Lee Kwan Yew and ended up going to China in the 50s. I'm an engineer so the Chinese put me to work building ports. I built ports all over China. Eventually, it just wasn't challenging anymore.

"Along the way I became friends with a minister here in Tanzania who came to China regularly. On one of his visits, I told him he had to find me a job here. My wife is Australian, and she has always wanted to see Africa."

He puffs on his cigarette and blows the smoke over his shoulder.

"And here I am."

"Sounds like an interesting way to get here."

And a pretty interesting life. Singapore. Communist China. Build ports. Australian wife. Come to Africa. But run a motor pool?

Li looks at me for a moment. "Come into to my office. You're a management consultant. You might be interested in something on my wall."

Li's office is small and cramped but there are a series of charts on the wall.

"This is a plot of the percentage of government vehicles in the Motor Pool each month. When I got here, fifty percent of all the vehicles were in the Motor Pool, most of them waiting for spare parts. Now it's down to 15 percent."

I look at the steadily dropping curve in the chart. Li shows me other charts that measure progress in output per hour, cost savings – the sort of stuff we would design for a McKinsey corporate client. I'm impressed.

Li takes me for a tour of the Motor Pool, chain smoking cigarettes as we go. He shows me the heavy equipment repair shop, the generator and starter motors rebuild shop, etc. He's obviously proud of his little empire. Everywhere we go, I see the same kind of efficient, hard-working mechanics that I saw in the service bay.

We come full circle back to the service area. My car has long been ready, and the mechanics are cleaning up for the day. It's not yet noon.

I turn to Li.

"Thanks for the tour. I'm impressed. But do you mind if I ask how you get people to work like they do here. It's, ah, not quite what I expect in Tanzania."

Li laughs.

"It's all about incentives. You have to give people incentives. I can't pay my guys more that the government-dictated wage. So I give them daily quotas, and when they're finished they go home. Most of these guys are working two jobs. What I'm doing is probably illegal, but what the hell? If the government finds out, they'll just send me back to China."

I stand there in the tropical sun for a moment, taking this all in. The one place in Tanzania that really works is run by a communist-leaning Chinese engineer who believes in incentives. Not 'from each according to his ability' but incentives. Pay for performance.

Then Li adds, "But Africa isn't like China. In Africa there are lots of resources but people don't know how to use them. China has far less resources per capita but people work hard and make the best use of what they have."

Li puffs on his cigarette and looks at me.

"Maybe we'll see each other again."

"I hope so."

Li has been a real bright spot in my Tanzanian experience. I climb into my car and drive off, pondering Li's comments about Africa vs. China and the need for incentives.

Marx thought Russia was not ready for communism. I begin to wonder whether Tanzania is ready for socialism. And I have this sinking feeling that lots of bright ideas and hard work — including mine — are going to run aground on the hard rocks of human nature before the Nyerere's dream of African socialism becomes reality.

In a way, I feel like I've been mugged. I thought that something new and better could emerge in Tanzania with its enlightened leadership and traditionally communal society mostly unaffected by imperialism and foreign capitalism. But it turns out to be a bit like an inspiring sermon — it sounds great, but what do you do on Monday morning? And then it's not a matter of big social or economic concepts, but about the choices and values and incentives that ordinary people hold or confront in their daily lives.

Ironic. I'm almost half way around the world from Idaho and human beings turn out to be basically the same everywhere. So why did I expect socialism to work in Tanzania when I could have easily predicted how it would work in Idaho? And why did it take a Chinese engineer in an African motor pool to teach me this lesson?

CHAPTER 36

Miriam and Mr. Sherrill

February, Dar Es Salam

"DON'T STAY UP TOO LATE, dear. You need to get better."

The sky is clear tonight and there's a full moon. Pam is just leaving to go on a midnight hack through the African countryside. I'm lying on the couch in the living room. It's a little before 9 pm.

"I had a long nap today. Just not sleepy yet."

She gives me a kiss and goes off down the hall, checking on the children, making sure the baby's mosquito net is still tucked in. A car pulls up in the driveway.

"Bye, dear. I love you."

"Have fun. I love you, too."

It's been a couple of weeks since I came down with the flu, and I'm still too weak to work full days. We've been in Tanzania nearly 6 months. Implementing the reorganization of the government has proven more difficult than any of the team imagined. Ironically, I'm in charge of the Ministry of Health and too sick to go to work.

Reading is about the only entertainment available in the house, and I have run out of things to read. I get up and wander over the bookcase to see if there's anything I have missed. I spot the modern translation of the New Testament that I gave Pam for Christmas. 'Nope, not that desperate.'

Then I come across the books Miriam sent after the family reunion last summer. They're basically the same ones she sent to Oxford three years ago. I pick up *They Speak with Other Tongues* by John Sherrill. I remember encouraging Pam to throw it away in Oxford, thinking the person who sent it must be some sort of religious fanatic. But last summer, Miriam and Doug seemed like normal people – rational, well-educated, successful professionals.

'What the hell. I'll give it a try.'

I lie back down on the couch and read the back cover. Sherrill is a journalist who writes for Guideposts magazine, which I have never read but recognize as being associated with Norman Vincent Peale, the Power of Positive Thinking guy who made such a stink about JFK's Catholicism. Not a very auspicious start. Still, I open the book.

Sherrill's story begins with a visit to his doctor in New York City, who tells him that the cancer in his back has returned and he needs a second surgery – immediately. Sherrill is a young man with young children. I can identify with the fear and gut level reaction to being told a life-threatening cancer still stalks him. Sherrill, who is only nominally a Christian, walks out of the doctor's office in Manhattan and dives into the first church he can find, "looking for darkness and privacy more than anything." He finds himself in a Lenten service with a short talk about Nicodemus.

"But you see," said the seminarian, "as long as Nicodemus was trying to come to an understanding of Christ through his logic, he could never succeed. It isn't logic, but an experience, that lets us know who Christ is."

Sherrill says this meant nothing to him at the time, but the next day a Christian friend tells him, "You're trying to approach Christianity through your mind... It simply can't be done that way. You have to be willing to experience it first, to do something you don't understand – and then oddly enough, understanding often follows." Later that day, Sherrill turns to his wife and says, "What do they call it: 'a leap of faith'? All right, I'm going to make the leap: I believe that Christ was God."

"It was a cold-blooded laying down of my sense of what was logical, quite without emotional conviction. And with it went something that was essentially 'me'. All the bundle of self-consciousness that we call our ego seemed somehow involved in this decision. It was amazing how much it hurt, how desperately this thing fought for life, so that there was a real kind of death involved. But when it was dead and quiet finally, and I blurted out my simple statement of belief, there was room in me for something new and altogether mysterious."

I stop reading and let the book drop onto my chest. The house is quiet. A small lizard moves across the living room wall, looking for mosquitoes. I hear the noises of the African night through the window screens and the *Askari* walking around the perimeter of the house.

'Experience not logic.' I struggle with the concept. Isn't the purpose of logic to analyze our experience, to provide consistency in how we view experience and to extract valid generalizations from it? I guess if I had recurrent cancer, I might be less picky. Logic isn't half as good as a warm blanket of experience on a cold night of fear and uncertainty.

I read on. Sherrill has the surgery, gets reassuring news from his surgeon, but finds himself in pain with two roommates who are also in pain. He tries prayer, for himself and for his roommates, "but it was like talking to the air over my bed." He goes to sleep but wakes in the middle of the night.

Fully awake, without transition from sleep. A little light came in from the hall and from the windows. A nurse passed the door on rubber-soled shores. Both of my roommates were restless, the one coughing, the other moaning softly.

I don't know how it was that I first became aware of the light. It was there, without transition, as my awakening had come. It was different from the light that came in through the door and window – more of an illumination than a light with a defined source. But there was something remarkable about this light; it had, somehow, a center of awareness. I was awed, but not at all afraid. Instead there was a sense of recognition, as if I were seeing a childhood friend, physically much changed so that what I recognized was a totality rather than a particular feature.

"Christ?" I said.

The light moved slightly. Not really moved; it was just suddenly closer to me without leaving where it was. I thought for a moment that the pain beneath my bandages was going away, but it did not. Something happened with that encounter, though. It was as if I were bursting with health through and through.

My roommates were still tossing, still coughing and groaning. "Christ," I said moving my lips only, " would you help that boy?" The light did not leave me, but in some strange way it was now at the bedside of the boy in pain. A little "Ohhh..." came from him and he was silent.

"And my other friend?" The light was instantly centered on the bed of the old man who was in the middle of a spasm of coughing. The cough stopped. The old man sighed and turned over.

And the light was gone.

Something stirs within me. I remember my Dad reading Psalms to me as a child. I had rheumatic fever when I was six and spent a summer confined to my bed. The core of Christian Science is the idea that sickness is an illusion. If you see the truly true truth about the really real reality, the sick will be healed.

But my Dad was a Christian Scientist of convenience; his roots were Lutheran and his approach to trouble was to turn to the Psalms. I remember the peace that came from his reading the 23rd and 91st Psalms. My Comfort God was born out of such experience. I wonder, 'how exactly did that work?'

Sherrill recovers from the surgery but the big spiritual experience fades. He wonders if that is all there is to Christianity. One big experience and then just the hard slog of 'faith'. A year later, he is asked by the Guideposts editors to meet with a Reformed minister by the name of Harald Bredesen who has an amazing story about being baptized in the Holy Spirit and speaking in tongues.

I stop reading again. *Um Gottes Willen!* For God's sake! I think back to a night in Austria when I first heard of this stuff from the Pentecostal evangelist on the ride from the German border to Vienna. Sherrill has me hooked.

They Speak with Other Tongues is about Sherrill's investigation into the origins of the Pentecostal movement and the spread of the experience of the baptism in the Holy Spirit into the mainline denominations in the 1950s and 1960s. It's a gripping tale. Sherrill starts researching for an article, then realizes it's really a book project. He proceeds the way a good journalist does – research, interviews, questioning, reflecting. I find that Sherrill's mind works very much like mine. Repeatedly, I get to the end of a chapter and think, 'Yes, but what about…?' and find that the next chapter addresses my question.

As I read, I am moved by the stories of people who experience God in amazing ways. Jesus is as real to them as their next-door neighbor. The Holy Spirit is a constant presence and source of inspiration, comfort and power. Miracles happen, people are healed; lives are changed – including, importantly, Sherrill's. I can't put the book down.

Sometime after midnight, Pam comes home from her ride and sees me on the couch.

"Honey, what are you doing up so late? You really need to get your sleep."

"It's OK, dear. I'm nearly finished with this book."

She comes over to the couch and gives me a kiss, but says nothing about the book. She knows me too well to try to turn me away from something once I'm into it.

Finally, around three in the morning, I finish the book. I feel drained. My emotions have been on a roller coaster all night. Multiple times, tears have welled up. It's a very happy book. And it stirs memories from Austria – the powerful sense of longing in Maria Laach, the peace of the

Ancient Austrian, the mystery of Christmas in Zell am See, the transition at Castel Grandolfo.

I get up and walk out to the kitchen. I drink some water, processing Sherrill's book. This is a different take on Christianity than anything I have encountered before. It's experiential. It seems real. It matches up with what you read in the New Testament. It has power. By comparison, the intellectualism and traditional liturgical forms of Christianity seem pallid and lifeless.

Sherrill's book challenges many of my preconceptions and prejudices. I think about it for a few minutes and then conclude that, if I were a Christian, I would want to have this experience. I would want the power and reality of the Holy Spirit. The tongues stuff is weird but I see how it fits in. But since I'm not a Christian, Sherrill's story is, in the end, not personally relevant.

Having thus processed and filed a night's reading, I walk down the hall, check again on the girls and crawl into bed with Pam.

Tomorrow's another day.

CHAPTER 37

A Narrow Escape

February, Nairobi

"HOW DO YOU LIKE THAT Bible?"

Dr. Bradley has spotted the copy of The Living Bible on my bedside table.

"I haven't had a chance to read it yet. The Chaplain left it there."

Bradley listens to my heart and lungs, then pokes my abdomen for the umpteenth time in a week.

"I think he's got Paul's letter to the Romans just right."

"Interesting," I reply. "I'll have to check it out."

It's been a week since I went to see Bradley. The plan was for the whole McKinsey team to fly to Arusha and then travel by Land Rover out to Kigomi on Lake Tanganyika to push along the recommended reorganization of the government in that region. And, incidentally, to make certain that the structure we had recommended made sense in the remoter parts of Tanzania.

Since I still wasn't feeling fully recovered from the flu, I flew up to Nairobi a couple of days ahead of the departure from Arusha in order to get a check up, there being no doctors left in Dar that I had any confidence in. I got Bradley's name from the insurance company that provides our healthcare coverage.

Bradley is a British physician who has been in Kenya most of his career. He looks the part. White hair, glasses, clear eyes, a kind face and an authoritative manner, he could be an English Marcus Welby.

After doing an initial work-up in his office, Bradley sits down at his desk and waits for me to get dressed. After a long pause, during which Bradley appears to be thinking while looking out the window, my curiosity gets the better of me.

"So, does this mean I'm cleared to travel out to Lake Victoria?"

Bradley looks at me with astonishment. "Travel? I'm trying to figure out how long you need to be in hospital. You're certainly in no shape to travel. The flu you thought you had was malaria, and I think you might also have amoebiasis."

The answer he came up with was a minimum of two weeks.

After a week of bed rest, I am starting to realize just how sick I was. I've regained a bit of weight, having tipped the scales at 124 pounds in Bradley's office. It's amazing what a good tan will cover up.

"So, how am I doing, Doctor?"

Bradley peers over his glasses at me.

"Much better. Your spleen is starting to shrink and your blood cell count is moving in the right direction. It was very good that you came to see me when you did. I don't think you would have survived the trip to Lake Victoria."

"Really? What makes you say that?"

"Well, your spleen was very distended and a trip in a Land Rover over unpaved roads would probably have ruptured it. Had that happened, most likely you would have died in the bush before anyone could get you to medical care. I think you've had a narrow escape."

Bradley says this in a matter fact way, but I can see that he is serious.

"I think it would be good for you to get up and walk around a bit. But not too much, just a stroll out to the garden now and then."

Bradley turns to leave, looks down at the Bible, then pauses by my bedside.

"My recommendation is that you get out of Africa. You've had a narrow escape. Once you've had malaria and amoebiasis, it's not good to stay exposed to tropical parasites. If you don't have to be in Africa, I think you should consider going back to the England or America as soon as you recover."

"Thank you, Doctor. I'll give it some thought."

"Do. And God bless you. See you tomorrow."

The prospect of a walk in the garden lifts my spirits. Nairobi Hospital is a series of low-rise buildings in a well-maintained tropical garden. I put on my bathrobe and wander down the hall to the nurse's station. I take along a biography of Cecil Rhodes that I picked off the book cart.

"Doctor Bradley said it was OK for me to take a walk."

The nurse directs me to the door out into the garden. Nairobi is essentially on the equator but more than a mile high, so the climate is mild and temperatures fairly constant year round. I sit on a bench in the sunshine and enjoy just being alive.

This isn't the way I expected my African adventure to end. I had planned on being in Tanzania at least a year, but Bradley's advice has shaken my determination to get back to work fixing the Tanzanian Government as soon as I start feeling better. Then a sense of irony overtakes me.

I think I came here with a sense of responsibility to the Rhodes Trust to do something good for Africa, a kind of roundabout payback to Africans from Cecil's gold and diamond profits. But reading his biography, here in my Nairobi Hospital bed, I get a better sense of the man and his vision for Africa. He thought on a continental scale and had enormous perseverance. His treks up through the heart of Africa involved lots of hard slogging and repeated bouts of malaria.

Knowing this about Rhodes adds to my sense of naiveté about my own plans to do something significant. Compared to my corporate finance engagements for European clients, the work in Tanzania has been largely ineffective and frustrating. There just doesn't seem to be a place for me to plug in what I know and who I am despite my desire to be involved in helping the global poor.

'A narrow escape.' Dr. Bradley's words keep running through my head.

I remember some other narrow escapes. Like the time when I was six and fell into a fast-flowing irrigation canal on a dark winter evening and managed to grab some bushes long enough for my brother and his friend to pull me out. Or my complete recovery from rheumatic fever. Or the time my friend rolled the truck we were in. I was thrown out and ended up under the truck with nothing but bruises and a hyper-extended elbow. Or the time I got stuck on the Interstate. Or the second brush with suicide on a bridge in Vienna.

Maybe the malaria and amoebiasis are – in a perverse sort of way – another narrow escape, this time from a misplaced sense of mission.

Funny, how life works. A fork in the road, a small variation in direction, a turn to the left rather than the right, a detour to Nairobi to see a doctor. One way is death, the other you get to live another day.

The Kenyan sky is incredibly blue. The sun is warm. My wife is coming to see me on the weekend. I have two wonderful daughters back in Dar. And I'm lucky to be alive.

"So there you are. The nurse told me I might find you out here."

I look up to see Pam coming down the walk. She sits down next to me and wraps me in one of her amazing hugs. We hold each other tightly for a long time.

"So, how are you feeling?"

"Better. Today is the first time I've been allowed to get out of bed."

"Wonderful. How would you like some company?"

"Terrific. Will they let you stay in my room?"

"Oh, no. I've got my own room. I stopped off to see Dr. Bradley's partner on the way here, and it looks like I have a serious case of amoebic hepatitis. I've just been admitted to the hospital. I'm in a room in the women's wing."

Pam smiles, but her expression belies the bundle of concerns that are now affecting us both – serious illness, the background stress of uncertainty and vulnerability that we experience in Tanzania, and the unclear prospects for recovery from parasitic diseases. The idea of having Pam in the hospital with me is comical in a way, but I can't decide whether to laugh or cry.

We sit for a long time on the bench, catching up on the girls and her visit to the doctor partner, what it means to have your liver invaded by parasites and the nature of the treatment. The sun starts to lower in the sky. Pam suggests that we go see what's on for dinner.

I get up from the bench and ponder the effects of the setting sun on the colors and shadows in the hospital's tropical garden. "I know what I would like – a great big, juicy American hamburger with fries and a milkshake."

Pam laughs. "And I suppose you think the Nairobi Hospital will just serve one up for you."

"Unlikely. But I think I know a place that will. The Intercontinental Hotel."

This is a guess on my part. The Vienna Intercontinental Hotel, which caters particularly to American tourists, was the one place in Vienna where you could get an authentic hamburger. Normally, I avoided the Intercontinental precisely because it was so American (and expensive). But occasionally my friends and I would indulge ourselves in a bit of Americana. I figure the Nairobi Intercontinental will have pretty much the same menu.

"But we're both in the hospital."

"It's alright. I bet we can sneak out and get a taxi downtown. What will they do if they find out? Discharge us in the middle of the night for bad behavior?"

Pam laughs again. "You're crazy. Too much time in the sun." But I see a conspiratorial, mischievous glint in her eye.

"Too much time in a hospital bed and not enough time with my wife."

My guess turns out to be right, and we savor our hamburgers like they were *fois gras* and *coq au vin*. We linger a long time in the bar of the Intercontinental, talking about our life together, about Oxford, London, Africa and about what we should do now. I tell Pam about Bradley's advice, and she tells me more about the doctor's recommended treatment.

"His advice is to go back to London for treatment at the Institute for Topical Diseases. Apparently, I have to take strychnine for at least a month."

"Strychnine? The poison?"

"Uh huh. It's apparently the best thing for killing the parasite."

I feel my stomach churn despite the feast of a lifetime that I have just eaten.

When I came to Africa, I thought of myself as doing something noble and good, something appropriate for a Rhodes Scholar who had been exempted from military service during a war. I knew Africa wasn't the best thing to do for a career in McKinsey, but I didn't expect it to have a cost in terms of Pam's – or even my – health. And, I realize that I need to rethink what I'm doing.

"You know, I really miss the States right now."

Pam laughs. "A good hamburger will do that to you."

I laugh with her. "That it will. But I don't feel like I'm in the right place. Dar wasn't working even when I was healthy. I think Africa is for Africans. They need to be the ones to figure out how to develop their resources and organize themselves. I'm not sure they want or need my advice. At least, not the sort of advice that I'm qualified to give at the moment."

Pam is quiet. I decide to change the subject before I ruin the evening.

"Just before you got here, I was thinking about how grateful I am to be alive. Bradley told me I had a narrow escape. I probably would have died in the bush if I hadn't stopped in Nairobi first."

"His partner told me the same thing."

"That started me thinking about what it means to be grateful. It's more than just being glad or feeling fortunate. It's like you're trying to say 'thank you' to someone or something. So, is this kind of feeling one of the sources of religious faith? Do people find – or invent – God at times of peace and joy, when they are grateful for the life they have? Are these little moments of gratitude experiences that prompt people to reflect and search and ask big 'why' questions?"

Pam runs the back of her arm across her forehead, as though she were wiping away sweat. "Whew. You expect me to answer questions like that on a full stomach?" She laughs.

"Okay, okay. Enough of being heavy and philosophical. I'm just grateful for you and the girls. And, of course, for a British doctor and a nice hospital in Nairobi. Even, believe it or not, for an Intercontinental Hotel."

We ride back up to the hospital, kiss each other good night in the main lobby and make our way back to our respective wings of the hospital. Walking down the hall, I ask myself again, 'why am I so lucky? Why have

I had such a narrow escape from death in the bush of Africa? Why didn't I die in that irrigation canal as a child? Why did I survive the car wreck as a teenager? Why did I get a Rhodes Scholarship?'

Why, indeed? And to whom should I be grateful? Chance? Fate? Or something more personal?

As I crawl into bed, I spot the Bible that the chaplain left next to my bed. Maybe I *should* read that Bible. Some day.

CHAPTER 38

When Atheists Pray

May, London

THEY SAY THERE ARE NO atheists in foxholes. I think the same is probably true for emergency rooms.

Pam and I are in the Kings College Hospital ER with Angela. A few hours earlier, on one of those rare occasions when I was in London working at my desk, I got the sort of call from Pam that you hope you never get. The stress in her voice was unforgettable. I could immediately tell that she was very emotional and just barely holding it together.

"Honey, I'm at the hospital with Angela. She fell down the stairs. I'm not sure she's going to live. Can you come?"

"How far did she fall?"

"From the top floor to the bottom. She went under the railing."

"Oh, God. What hospital are you in?"

"Kings College. Hurry. Please."

"I'll be there right away."

I jump in a taxi and head for the hospital. My mind is racing with fear, imagining what happened to Angela, what I'm likely to find at the hospital, and how we will deal with a worst-case outcome – possible permanent disability or even death. I'm pretty sure I know how it happened.

And it's my fault.

In the end, I took Bradley's advice and left Tanzania. The London office promptly assigned me to an organizational effectiveness study for the Irish Ministry of Health. Our house was Dulwich was still rented out, so I sent Pam and the girls to the States for a month and headed for Dublin.

Our house is a modern townhouse design with lots of glass and open space to allow as much light into the house as possible. The stairway is in the middle of the house, with two flights of stairs per floor. There is an open well down the middle, to allow light to reach the ground floor. The flaw in the stairway design, however, is that the guardrail consists of a single wide board running parallel to the banister. This works fine for adults, but it leaves a space under the guardrail that a small child can easily slide through.

I noticed the problem with the staircase a few weeks ago when we finally moved back into the house. Angela is about to start walking and loves climbing the stairs and going down again. I could see that I needed to put up some sort of fence to prevent her from accidentally going under the railing.

But I just haven't gotten around to it yet.

I find Pam in the ER waiting room. She's on the edge of tears.

"Angela's in X-ray. It's all my fault."

I wrap my arms around her, and she starts crying.

"What happened?"

"I was on the top floor making the beds. Angela was crawling around after me. I guess she tried to go down the stairs and went under the rail. She fell down through the middle. I heard her hit the banisters on the way down and then hit the floor at the bottom. I ran downstairs expecting to find her dead. I put her in the car and drove her to the hospital. It doesn't look good. She threw up in the car.

"I should have been watching her. It's all my fault."

"It's not, Honey. I saw the problem with the railings weeks ago. I should have fixed it."

We both realize this isn't the time to sort out who's to blame. We both failed. And now our baby is horribly injured.

We sit down, holding hands, not speaking.

I guess people pray for all kinds of reasons. It isn't the sort of thing Pam and I have ever done together, other than in a church service. So we both do it now in our own ways, silently. I reach back into my childhood – the Psalms I memorized in Sunday school, the Lord's Prayer, other things I picked up in Christian Science and my Catholic explorations. I remember my Dad reading the Bible when I was sick. I remember, in particular, the 23rd Psalm: 'Yea, though I walk through the valley of the shadow of death, thou art with me.'

'Lord, have mercy. Heal Angela. Do a miracle.'

A doctor steps into the waiting room. "Mrs. Bock?"

We walk over to him, fearing, hoping. I introduce myself.

"Your baby has a fracture of the skull but no other broken bones. She's severely concussed and her head is starting to swell quite badly. We won't know for a few hours just how serious the swelling is going to be. But she's asleep and stable for now. We plan to keep her in the hospital overnight for observation. We're transferring her to a room upstairs. You can come and see her now."

He says all of this in a calm and measured way. We both heave a sign of relief. At least she's alive, and so far, so good.

We go up to the room. Angela is in a bed, sleeping. Her forehead is badly swollen and turning black and blue. Otherwise, she's in remarkable shape. We sit by her bedside, waiting, watching.

Eventually, she opens her eyes and sees us. The 'Ma-ma' and 'Da-da' are weak but so sweet to hear. We hold her little hands and gently stroke her, both of us wavering ridiculously between laughter and tears.

After a little while, Angela wants to get out of the bed. She has always been an incredibly active child – adventuresome, people oriented and seemly always awake during the day. Pam calls her, 'the incredible, non-sleeping baby.' True to form, now she wants to get up and play.

But she's weak and groggy, so we carry her around a bit and then sit her on the bed. A nurse appears to check on her and goes off to get her some juice to drink. The juice arrives in a British-style Sippy cup, which we recognize is not going to work for Angela. Pam takes the lid off the cup, sets the lid on the bed, and then holds the cup so Angela can drink out of it.

Then something happens that would mean very little to anyone other than Pam and me. Angela reaches down, picks up the lid, and puts it back on the Sippy cup.

We both laugh. We laugh the way you laugh when something really, really wonderful happens to you.

Because we see in this little action that Angela is absolutely fine. We know her as an adventuresome, extroverted, intelligent child who is always figuring out new things. The fact that she has instantly figured out the connection between the lid and the cup tells us that her mind is working just the way it always has.

I heave another sigh of relief. I start to say, 'we are so, so lucky' but then I catch myself.

Once again, I find my life peculiarly intertwined with this baby. Her birth quickened a sense of the miraculous in me. Her christening strangely bonded us together in a common experience of faith and ceremony. And now her survival of a potentially fatal fall follows closely on my own narrow escape a few months before in the plains of Africa.

This seems like something far more mysterious than luck.

I feel the tug of memories of other times when this *mysterium tremendum et fascinans* seemed to draw near – Maria Laach, for instance, standing on a bridge in Vienna, overlooking the Castel Grandolfo in Rome, at a dinner in Oxford.

Maybe this is how disasters work, at least sometimes. They make you stop and think about something other than what to eat or what to wear or how you're going to get ahead in the world. They strip you down and give you a chance to weigh up what is *really* important to you.

I have traveled a long way since that conversation with Lydia, from Utah to Vienna to Seattle to Oxford to London to Africa, and now back to London. Along the way, I've acquired a wife and two daughters, whom I love deeply. Overall life is good. But the quest that started out in Utah still seems incomplete.

I started out looking for a secular, post-Christian culture in Europe, but instead found myself in a quest for understanding of spiritual things. Then in Oxford, when I found the El Dorado of skepticism, it was too late for me to really embrace a thoroughgoing public atheism a la Marx. My Vienna experience left me with a respect, even admiration, for Christianity and the culture that it created. Then came Pam and Heather and Angela and profound experiences of love and life and narrow escapes.

The reluctant atheist has become wistful, mellowed and even more reluctant.

The Oxford to Africa scene in the adventure movie plays out. Again the hero has hiked up a hill, looked over the top and been disappointed. Worse, he lost his footing at the top of the ridge and tumbled back down the hill, bouncing from rock to rock. Bruised and battered, he camps beside a dry streambed. 'No more El Dorado stuff,' I tell myself. 'Stay away from the quicksand and watch out for the python. Just sit here and concentrate on staying alive.'

For a while anyway.

Part Three

CHAPTER 39

An All-Round Friend

Early September, Washington DC

IT'S LATE ON A WEDNESDAY night, and I'm looking out my office window at the passing traffic on Pennsylvania Avenue while I try to figure out how to phrase a recommendation in a client presentation due Friday. I've been in McKinsey's DC office for a bit more than a year. One of the partners landed an assignment for the Secretary of Commerce and put out an APB for associates with a background in international economics. I arrived in DC on July 4th, expecting to return to London in the fall.

It turned out that Arch Edwards had a hand in my DC assignment. He rotated back to DC from London about two years ago to start a US health care practice and asked me to stay on to help him develop it. Given the opportunity to do something significant in a key sector of the economy and make a contribution to public policy, I agreed to stay in DC for two years. This evening I'm trying to come up with a one-page version of a national healthcare strategy using the infamous McKinsey matrix.

I hear a light knock on the open door behind me and swivel around to see Scott quietly waiting to get my attention.

"Looks like you're burning the midnight oil again," he says.

"Ah yes, welcome to the life of a McKinsey associate – something I hear you've decided to escape. Tell me again what it is you're going to do?"

The question is disingenuous. Scott is a couple of years senior to me and recently announced his resignation at the end of the summer. People leaving McKinsey after four years are not unusual. 'The Firm', as insiders know it, provides a great stepping-stone to a career in business. But Scott doesn't have a place to go, and I know it. He has simply resigned. Everyone knows he is too good at his job and too talented to have been forced out. A simple resignation thus challenges the culture and leadership of the Firm. Late on a Wednesday night with a presentation that refuses to come together, I'm secretly envious.

"TBD."

"You're not worried? You must have a rich uncle."

Scott laughs. He's tall, good-looking, Stanford undergrad and student body president, Harvard MBA, Vietnam vet and numerous other distinctions. He's also warm, friendly and kind – a guy I would like to have as a friend – but now he's leaving for an undetermined destination.

Scott and his wife Ruth are also gracious, friendly people who manifest a sincere interest in others. Pam and I met Ruth at a DC office retreat in the early fall. She's tall like Scott, someone whose quiet warmth makes you immediately comfortable in her presence.

Scott comes into my office and leans against the credenza.

"Now that would be nice," he says in a very relaxed way. "Unfortunately not. I resigned in what you might call a 'step of faith'. I believe that the Lord will show me what the next thing is when I'm ready for it and when it's ready for me."

I rock back in my chair, studying Scott's face. Scott has a reputation around the office for being religious. In fact, he's the only McKinsey associate I know who has a Bible on his credenza. And I have been in a lot of McKinsey offices – London, Paris, Amsterdam, Dusseldorf, New York, San Francisco, LA, Chicago, etc. 'Sorry, no Bibles here. We don't do religion or talk about it. We're fact-based and analytical.'

"Any idea what that will be? Thinking about going into the ministry?"

Scott laughs again.

"No, I tried that already. It wasn't for me. I'm a business guy and looking for the right spot where I can make a contribution."

"Interesting."

One of the things I've learned in my brief business career is to always go to the other guy's office when you want to keep the conversation short. That way, you control how long the meeting lasts. When you think it's finished, you simply walk out the door. Particularly when you have a lot of work to do.

Tonight, however, Scott and I are in *my* office, and he's settled in on my credenza. I decide to make the best of the situation by establishing some common ground with Scott that I can use later on to maintain a relationship. Or at least keep track of how his 'step of faith' works out. You can never have too many talented people in your network. I decide to relate on Scott's turf.

"My wife has an aunt and uncle who would probably understand what you're doing. They talk about being led by the Holy Spirit and how the Lord shows them things. They have some interesting stories about how that has worked out in their lives and in their friends lives."

"And what do you think, David?"

"I don't know them well. Only met them once, a couple of years ago. They're serious about their faith. Pam's uncle is a retired Air Force Colonel, her aunt is a linguist. But 'on the fringe', as far as I can tell."

"Why do you say that?"

"Well, they claim to speak in tongues and pound the drum for an experience they call being baptized in the Holy Spirit. A couple of years ago, they sent us a book called *They Speak with Other Tongues*. I read it, thought it was interesting, but not really relevant to me. Good to understand where your crazy in-laws are coming from, though."

I smile at Scott, thinking I'm hitting the right notes in relating to a sophisticated guy who believes in God. Scott smiles back, still leaning against the credenza.

"You know, David, I've had that experience myself."

Suddenly, all the air in the room disappears.

"Really?"

I say it as carefully as possible, trying to convey interest and respect. But like the proverbial duck who's calm above the water but paddling like mad, I'm not sure what to do next. Scott is what Cecil Rhodes would have called an 'all-rounder,' but in Scott's case the all-rounding includes a deep religious faith and experience.

I realize I have really put my foot into it with the 'fringe' comment about the Holy Spirit. My prior encounters with this religious phenomenon have been with people largely outside my intellectual and professional world. But now the 'Holy Ghost' has invaded my McKinsey office in downtown Washington DC, brought by a guy who is every bit my peer if not superior. Scott is not someone whose experience I can easily dismiss, even if I'm not quite sure what it is.

"Amazing," I say as sincerely as I can. "You know, Scott, I would really like to hear more about this. But I've got to get this presentation done. How about dinner sometime soon with the wives?"

"Sounds great." Scott stands up to leave. "I'll talk to Ruth and we'll set something up. Don't stay here too late. Remember that when you're old and gray and in the retirement home, your children just might come and visit you. Your clients certainly won't."

We both laugh, and I turn back to my presentation.

Two hours later, still thinking about the conversation with Scott, I crawl into bed with Pam. I'm exhausted and hoping for a few hours sleep before the children get up and I go back to the office. She turns over and wraps a sleepy arm around me. I feel the soft warmth of her body against mine.

"How was work? Get your presentation done?"

We've done this so many times, I'm pretty sure she's asking the questions in her sleep.

"Yeah, got it done. But you'll never guess what I found in the office today."

I slide over into her embrace and begin thinking maybe I'm not so tired after all.

"What was that?" comes the sleep-talking response.

"Scott – y'know, of Scott and Ruth?

"Mmmm…"

He's one of those baptized-in-the-Holy-Spirit-type Christians like your Aunt Miriam."

"What!" Pam sits up in bed, suddenly wide-awake. "What did you say?"

"I said Scott is a baptized-in-the-Holy-Spirit Christian. At least I think he is."

"He is? What about Ruth? Is she as well? How did you find this out?"

"He told me. And I don't know about Ruth. But I can't imagine that he is and she isn't."

Pam flops back down in bed. "How did you ever get onto this subject in the office?"

"He wandered into my office, I asked him what he was planning to do, he said something about God, and I started telling him about your Aunt Miriam and Uncle Doug. I thought he would find it a bit amusing. But then he said, 'I've had that same experience myself.' I'm not sure what he meant. It could have been that he was a serious Christian. But I took it to mean that he is like Miriam and Doug. I didn't follow up, because I didn't want to get into a long discussion with him, and he didn't push it. I just thought you might be interested."

Pam is quiet for a while. I turn over and start drifting off to sleep.

"Honey, there's something I need to tell you."

The tone of her voice indicates that we are about to have a serious conversation. I struggle back from near sleep and turn on a light to help keep me awake. Pam is propped up on one elbow in the bed.

"Ok, fire away."

"You remember the book that Aunt Miriam sent us in Africa, the one about speaking in tongues?"

"Uh, yeah, I think so."

In fact, I remember it all too well, but have never discussed it with Pam. I realize now that she may be unaware of the fact that I read it. Now is clearly not the time to tell her.

"When I read it, I understood my grandmother's world for the first time."

"You mean the one you used to travel around with? The preacher?"

"Yes. My Dad had forbidden her to ever take me into one of her meetings or to talk to me about religion, so I really didn't know what it was she did. But when I read Sherrill's book, I realized that Granny was a Pentecostal evangelist."

"Interesting."

And complicated. In one day, the Holy Spirit thing has invaded both my office and my bed.

"So, have you followed up with Miriam or anyone about it?"

"No." I detect some hesitation in her voice.

"Why not?"

"Because I'm a bit afraid of how you would react. I know how you feel about religion. And I don't want it to come between us."

At other points in my life, I would not have found it acceptable to have a wife who is interested in religion, let alone one active in it. Tonight I don't particularly care. Part of it is being tired and preoccupied with career and family. Part of it is because life and experience have cooled the atheist passions. I'm still officially a reluctant atheist, but now I guess a *mellowed* reluctant atheist.

"Honey, I'm happy for you if you want to pursue it. I'm OK doing Christmas and christenings and weddings. But I'm not interested in taking on all the duties and constraints that religion involves. I'll tag along, but it's not for me."

"You sure?"

"Yeah, I'm sure."

I turn off the light and start drifting back to la-la land.

"Honey, can we have Scott and Ruth over for dinner sometime?"

"Mmm... yeah. Scott was going to talk to Ruth..."

Somewhere between sleep and consciousness, I have a flashback to the jungle adventure movie. I'm back in the dry riverbed, having twice failed to find El Dorado. The clothes are tattered, the shoes worn. And it's starting to rain. Small rivulets of water are forming in the river, and I begin to realize that this is not a safe place. The rain becomes heavier. The river starts to flow and high canyon walls surround me. Do I turn and run? Or just sit here, hoping for the best?

The last thing I hear is something about, "I think I'll call Ruth tomorrow."

CHAPTER 40

Time and Money

Late September, Bethesda

PAM AND I ARE IN the car on our way to a cocktail party at some friends' house in Virginia. As we head down the hill from our neighborhood to Mass Avenue, Pam asks, *apropos* of nothing,

"Honey, what do you really think about this God business?"

For some reason, I don't find the question surprising or out of place. I know Pam has been reading books on Christianity for the last few weeks, ever since she got in touch with Ruth following my conversation with Scott.

One Sunday afternoon, we happened to be driving in Scott and Ruth's neighborhood, and Pam insisted we stop so she could borrow another book. I offered to stay in the car with the girls while Pam went up to the door, sort of like the father who drives the family to church and then sits in the car and smokes a cigarette. Scott and Ruth were way too gracious for that and insisted that we all to come in while Pam went through Ruth's bookshelf of Christian books – which was extensive.

I stayed away from the books and engaged Scott in a business discussion to prevent anyone from getting the idea that I wanted to talk about religion. Nonetheless, their warm hospitality reminded me of other times and places where Christians welcomed me despite my wary behavior.

This evening, however, the phrase 'this God business' triggers a connection between work I have done on risk in capital budgeting and some further processing of the conversation with Scott in my office. I come up with a one-sentence reply to Pam's question.

"I think the downside risks of not believing are rather large."

This off the cuff, flippant answer seems to satisfy Pam. Or, maybe it just stops a conversation before it can get started.

One side of me is happy to cut off conversation about religion. While I'm less hostile to the subject than I was a decade ago, I'm apprehensive about where Pam's interest might take her and what it would mean for our relationship. I really, really don't want to get entangled in religion. But I'm also feeling drawn to the transcendental side of life. And, I'm finding that the memories of Maria Laach and lots of other encounters with people about the mysteries of the universe have been stirred up by the conversation with Scott and Pam's rekindled interest in spiritual things.

Ever since high school, the 'God business' has always been one of facts, logic and necessity.

Is belief in God necessary to explain the world around us?

Are religious convictions true based on verifiable evidence?

What is the syllogism whose conclusion is: 'Therefore, God exists'?

In my view, there are no convincing, i.e., non-disprovable, philosophical arguments for the existence of God. In the philosophical paradigm, religious belief can never be more than a leap of faith, a willful suspension of the ground rules of rationality.

Against this, there is the experience of people who have religious faith like Scott. What weight, if any, should I give to such stories?

In one of my more 'open' moments, when I was sick and weak in Africa, I read Sherrill's book on Pentecostalism. One of the Sherrill's comments that stuck awkwardly in me was the idea that you can't come to Christianity through the intellect. You have to experience Christ and then the intellect follows. Moreover, I think about the people I have met over the last decade who have had religious experiences, particularly of the Pentecostal/Charismatic kind. I guess I have to treat these experiences as facts, albeit facts that are capable of more than one interpretation.

I have largely ignored these facts, on the grounds that they were distant from me and not relevant. But with Scott, they are drawing nearer to me and are harder to ignore or dismiss. And if I can't ignore or dismiss them, then I'm going to have to make a decision about their truth and their application to me.

The thought occurs to me that this is quite similar to a business decision under conditions of uncertainty, and I begin to see the fallacy in some of my philosophical arguments about the existence of God.

If I have learned anything in McKinsey, it is the importance of fact-based decision making. The art of management is to be both fact-based *and* decisive. You don't have the luxury of infinite time or resources, particularly in major capital investments. So you gather enough information to reduce risk to acceptable levels and analyze the distribution of possible outcomes – the 'upside' and the 'downside'.

Then you make a decision.

I've always believed that there is a logical answer for all of the issues that religious experience throws up. Given enough time, science will explain it all to us. There are no mysteries in life, only things yet to be explained.

The problem, I now see, is that *I* don't have unlimited resources or time to wait for the answers. I only have one life to live, one death to die. The existence of God may not be so much the conclusion of a syllogism, whose major and minor premises need to be filled in, but a decision to be made under conditions of uncertainty.

For Christians, the upside is heaven, the downside hell. And the decision to be made is how to invest your time and your life. Neither option is free.

Based on what I've seen in Christianity, heaven can have a high cost in terms of the here and now. It's why I backed away from becoming a Catholic priest and hence a Christian – lots of sacrifice, lots of rules to keep, and a pretty dreary existence for the most part.

Hell, by comparison, requires less investment, but offers a highly negative payoff. In fact, in the Christian view of the world, the downside risk of not believing is infinite.

I thought I had put these troubling philosophical questions behind me. I'm not looking for El Dorado any more. I've settled down beside the rocky streambed and built a camp. It's not what I set out to find, but it's comfortable in a way, and it seems to be free of pythons and quicksand.

Unfortunately, my ever-faithful companion has developed gold fever and is now dragging me along in her own quest for El Dorado.

CHAPTER 41

The Downpour

Late October, Washington DC

"WE'RE DELIGHTED THAT YOU COULD make it on such short notice."

We've just arrived for dinner at Scott and Ruth's house in Northwest DC, and Scott's greeting at the door is warm and heart felt. It's an untypically warm October evening. The windows are open and a gentle breeze blows through the house as we enter.

This is our second dinner with Scott and Ruth in as many weeks. The first time was at our house. It was a fun evening and we're very much enjoying the budding friendship and wish we had done it sooner, but afterwards Pam was disappointed that the conversation never got around to the subject of religion. As for me, I failed to notice the lack of religious discussion.

Ruth appears out of the kitchen with a big smile and discrete but warm hugs for us both.

"Welcome to our house. We're so delighted you could come at the last minute."

Given how tall Ruth is, we both have to stretch for the hug.

"Let me introduce you to our friend Tru who is visiting from California and staying with us for a few days."

Ruth guides us into the living room.

Tru is another fairly tall and attractive woman, with highlighted blond hair, big bangs, and very trendy clothes. We shake hands.

"It's very nice to meet you. Ruth has told me a bit about the two of you. I'm looking forward to getting to know you better."

Tru's greeting is warm but reserved. Her smile is soft and her face conveys sensitivity mixed with sincere interest in other people. She strikes me as someone with a lot of depth, probably based on a tender heart and a lot of experience with hurting people. The focus in her blue-green eyes is intense and a bit unsettling.

We sit down and Scott serves the drinks as we go through the usual 'how did you meet, how did you get here' stuff. I discover that Ruth is also from California, and she and Tru have been friends for a long time. Scott and Ruth both laugh easily and smile a lot. The hospitality is gracious and the friendship genuine.

Despite the easy banter and fun, there's something inside me that begins to tighten up. While I want to be supportive of Pam, I am not interested in getting into a religious conversation myself. And, there are elements of the evening – e.g., the lack of alcohol – that unwittingly take me back to my Idaho roots and my cynicism about religion.

The Cynic in me begins to assess how the evening might progress. There are three serious Christians, one curious person, and one mellowed atheist. At least I'm not the one in the hot seat.

At 7:30 sharp, Ruth announces that dinner is served and we move to the dining room. Scott is at one end of the table, with Pam on his right and Ruth on his left. I'm at the other end of the table with Ruth on my right and Tru on my left next to Pam. It looks like a safe place to be. Scott puts out his hands towards Pam and Ruth and says, "Shall we pray?" We all join hands in a simple blessing, something that briefly evokes memories of wonderful meals together with friends in Vienna.

As we begin eating, Scott turns to Pam. "Ruth tells me you've been doing a lot of reading lately. What's your favorite new book?"

Pam hesitates before answering, then decides to keep her answer light and funny.

"I found 'The Hiding Place' very moving. In fact, I felt a bit silly reading it. It's been such nice weather that I decided to read in the Dumbarton Oaks garden in Georgetown. So I went to the French Market, bought a pate' sandwich and a split bottle of wine, and read the book on a park bench. I sort of sobbed my way through it."

Pam laughs her wonderful laugh, and everyone else joins in at the thought of a sophisticated young woman crying over a book in the middle of Georgetown.

"No place to hide," I quip, and everyone laughs again.

Ruth then turns to me. "Scott tells me that you've read 'They Speak with Other Tongues'. I'm curious to know what you thought."

I realize that Ruth is just showing friendly curiosity, but a knot starts to form in my stomach. I can see that I've made the mistake of joining a conversation about religion. 'Damn,' I think, 'let's see if I can be supportive and friendly without drawing any more attention to myself.'

"I found it interesting history. I liked Sherrill's approach and the way his mind works. Given the title, I didn't expect it to be as well written and logical as it was. In fact, the first time I saw the book, I threw it in the trash thinking it was about snake handlers in Appalachia."

I laugh to show I'm only half serious, and I get a chuckle out of Scott.

"I'm curious to know what effect it had on you," says Tru.

I think for a minute, then decide that I should probably stay on topic for another minute or two before steering the conversation in another direction.

"Actually, it was a bit like Pam and The Hiding Place. We were in Tanzania. I was recovering from malaria, and it was the only book in the house I hadn't read. I started reading it about nine in the evening and finished about three in the morning."

"You read it in one sitting?" says Scott. "That's impressive!"

"I think Pam read it at the same time."

I offer this information to get the focus shifted back to the reason I'm here at all. But Tru wants to know more.

"What was it about the book that captivated you like that?"

"'Captivated' would be too strong of a word. It interested me and showed me an aspect of Christianity that I knew very little about. It wasn't the tongues stuff that intrigued me but the power of the Holy Spirit that

Sherrill describes. I decided that if I were a Christian, I would want to have that sort of spiritual life. But since I'm not a Christian, in the end what Sherrill describes just isn't relevant for me."

Ruth is quiet for a moment. "Have you ever thought about asking for it?"

She smiles sweetly. I give Pam a plaintive look. Unfortunately, she seems to be enjoying watching me squirm.

"Ah, if only it were so simple, Ruth. At one time in my life, I thought long and hard about religious belief. For whatever reason, I'm either not able or not willing to take that leap of faith."

Ruth smiles at me. I scramble to think of a way to get out of the spotlight in the dinner conversation. Tru starts to say something, but I cut her off.

"Pam, however, is very interested. You know, her grandmother was an early time Pentecostal evangelist."

"No kidding," says Scott. "Tell us about her."

Mission accomplished. Whew.

Pam talks about her grandmother, then about her aunt and uncle and answers lots of questions about her own search for deeper spiritual experience in her life. I check my watch under the table. We should be able to politely excuse ourselves in the not too distant future.

Over dessert, Tru turns to me again.

"David, I've been thinking about what you said earlier about faith. And I'm wondering if you might be approaching the issue the wrong way."

Ouch! I know Tru is being incredibly sincere in her interest, but the question stirs up the Cynic and a lot of memories of a frustrating (and frustrated) search for meaning and truth many years ago.

Tru looks at me to see how I might be reacting. I keep a poker face, but am a little bit annoyed by the comment. After all, I'm a Rhodes Scholar with a degree in philosophy. I know Tru means well, but the Cynic still thinks of philosophy as basically a male preserve. 'Now,' (says the Cynic), 'I have a Southern California girl with streaky blond hair and bangs telling me I might be wrong about an issue that preoccupied me during a period when I was intensively studying philosophy.'

I keep quiet, so Tru continues.

"God is a person and he has created us in his image and likeness. That means we also have personality, and the freedom to choose what we believe and how we will live. God has created us this way because he loves us and wants us to love him in return. But love is always free. If we were compelled to love him, if we had no choice, then it wouldn't be love. He never forces himself on us. So it's not a matter of logic, but of a free choice to accept God's love and walk with him. If it were just a matter of reason and logic, only the very smartest would get to heaven. But God always leaves us the option of not choosing him."

As Tru says this, she's smiling but her eyes are searching my face looking for a reaction. As near as I can tell, I'm succeeding in revealing nothing. My face is expressionless, as they say. But Tru's sincerity and concern for me is palpable. Something inside me starts to stir.

Can it really be this simple? After all the analysis and logic and debate and rationalizing, does this 'God business' just come down to a simple *choice*? I feel the basis of my philosophical atheism being undercut, like the foundations of a house in a flood. The walls start to crack, the roof comes loose, and the water rises higher.

It is only through a conscious effort of will that I manage to keep the house from collapsing altogether. The Cynic says, 'Careful, David. Don't let your emotions get out of control. You need to keep the discussion on a rational level.' After a bit of tamping down, the emotion fades again.

"Tru, all choices are rational in some sense. Even love. The question is how rational they are and what tests we use to verify the truth of what we choose. Logic and epistemology are key to making the right choices, especially when it comes to our basic view of the world. My problem with religious faith is that it is so subjective. In science, truth is objective and provable. I think the same thing should be true for all our knowledge. If God exists, then it should be knowable to any rational person. If it's a matter of emotion, then you're on a very slippery slope."

Tru continues to look at me with that peculiar mix of pain and concern. I'm not sure what's going on in her mind. I'm guessing that I have put her down in unnecessarily harsh terms. But I'm wrong, and Tru's incredibly patient and persevering response catches me off guard.

"David, I think you're trying to answer the question of God's existence for everyone else. But what matters is the answer you give for yourself. Everyone else in the world may be wrong. You may be the only person who gets it right. But the only person who can answer for you is you."

It isn't what I was expecting. My first reaction is to try to counter Tru's argument. I start running through the supposed proofs of God's existence and their refutations to see which one best fits this situation. Then I realize that the whole exercise is futile.

Not just because Tru appears to be undeterred by my supposed intellectual brilliance. But because what she says is, well, *true*. I have a flashback to Oxford and the Vicar's counsel about marriage. Love is a choice, a commitment. That conversation shaped my relationship with Pam. The analogy here is that, if the Christian concept of God is true, then the only rational response is to commit to him, to choose to love him as he (supposedly) loves me.

This line of thinking sets off something akin to a war inside me.

On the one hand, the Cynic keeps reminding me that atheism is the only truly rational worldview. On the other, I am having another one of those experiences of being pulled against my will into the mystery of life, its randomness, its brevity, its beauty and its transcendence. It's these experiences that have turned me from the evangelical atheist of early college years to the reluctant atheist sitting here at a dinner party in Washington DC. And as in Maria Laach and a dozen other places many years ago, I'm being pulled by a desire for transcendence and meaning into something larger than myself.

Suddenly, the emotions inside are really raging, and I feel on the verge of completely losing control. My mind races. For a moment, I am caught up with the idea of doing something seriously foolish and stupid, like kneeling down on the floor with these friends and praying. About what I don't know. But I want what these people have. I'm in Vienna and Rome and Dar Es Salaam and a dozen other places where this cosmic longing for life and meaning has overtaken me.

Finally, I take a deep breath and compose a response.

"I see what you're saying, Tru. In fact, I was thinking the other day that belief in God is a bit like making a business decision under conditions of uncertainty. You get enough information to make a rational choice and then you choose. I'll give it some further thought."

This seems to mollify Tru. I feel the emotion drain away. The table conversation shifts to other things. I feel relieved, then tired, then frustrated with myself for letting my emotions nearly get the best of me, which then naturally shifts to irritation with Tru for her well-meant attention.

But the emotional stirring is gone. Inwardly, I feel coldly rational again. I hear a little voice saying, 'I need to get out of here, and I have no interest in seeing these people again any time soon, if ever.' The Cynic is back in control. I look at my watch again, this time above the table.

"Hon, it's pretty late. I think we'd better be going. The babysitter needs to get home. Scott, Ruth, it's been a very interesting evening and you have been wonderful hosts. Thank you very much. Tru, I've enjoyed our little conversation."

I smile as graciously as I can and start to stand up. Before I can get to my feet, Ruth says, "Scott, I think we should pray before they go." Scott extends a hand in each direction. "Yes, let's do that." We close the circle for Scott's benediction. 'Not my thing,' I think, trying to focus on being polite and going home.

But I can sense the python slithering across the floor towards my chair.

Then Scott looks at me and says softly, "David, why don't you just follow me?"

The question is ambiguous and capable of being interpreted either as an invitation to add something to the benediction, or to do what I think Scott is really getting at, which is to pray for myself.

I look at Scott, and realize that I have perhaps five or ten seconds to figure out what I'm going to do.

There are two options: I could say no and risk offending three people who have been wonderful hosts and friends, not to mention embarrassing my wife, and have to spend time explaining to them why I can't or don't want to participate in their world. Or, I could accept Scott's invitation, say a quick prayer, and get out the door.

At one time, this would have been an easy answer: just say no. But Scott's invitation is so gentle and sincere, so much a reflection of his professionalism and friendship that I can't muster the old hardline atheist response. Besides, saying no will further delay my getting out of this conversation and away from the approaching python.

I opt for the quick exit.

Scott begins, "Lord Jesus…"

So I say, "Lord Jesus…"

Scott continues, "I confess that I am a sinner and have need of a savior…"

But I'm not with him. In fact, I can't speak.

Somewhere, way, way up river, a dam breaks, and I am suddenly in the middle of the flood. An emotional wall of water hits me, and I am totally overwhelmed. In a moment, the cold, cynical rationality is swept away. I start to cry, then sob uncontrollably, tears streaming down my face.

I'm not sure how this looks to the others. It has probably taken them by surprise as well. In any event, there is no prospect of my regaining control. The flood has been released and it sweeps me with it.

Scott tries to resume the prayer, but then realizes that something profound has happened to me. He and Ruth and Tru just sit there quietly, still holding hands in a circle, while the weight of heaven crashes down over my head. I start trying to figure out how the words 'Lord Jesus' could trigger such an amazing, unexpected response.

At the moment, the only explanation I can think of is that I have *come home*. At least, that's what it feels like. Years of hurt and pain and loneliness and alienation are being swept away in the flood. Like the Prodigal Son, I have returned to my father's house. More than that, I have been *transported* there. One moment, I'm sitting in the pigsty. The next I'm being embraced and kissed. And that great cosmic desire is being fulfilled, that powerful longing for meaning and significance is finally being satisfied.

Amazingly, all of this is triggered by uttering two simple words — hypocritically, cynically and just to bring a dinner party to an end. This doesn't remotely comply with any of the requirements of religious belief as I understand them. But I know — feebly and imperfectly — that I am in the presence of something larger than myself, something ancient, deep and transcendent.

In the flash of an eye, I have gone from being coldly rational to a blubbering idiot. All I can say through the tears and overwhelming emotion of the moment is, "There is nothing I need to be anymore, nothing I need to be."

I can sense that this means nothing to the others, but to me this statement sums up the feeling of affirmation — or is it love? — that has overtaken me. I don't need to *be* anybody. Because I *am* somebody. In this moment, I am the most loved person in the world. Love is pouring over me and washing away years of alienation and striving to be accepted, perfect, better than anyone else.

It doesn't matter anymore who I am to others. I have come home.

I cry for a long time. Eventually, the tears stop, someone hands me a box of tissues and I begin to reassemble myself. A deep sense of peace comes over me. I just want to sit for a moment and steep in it. Scott and Ruth and Tru seem to understand. Pam is very quiet. Something deep and wonderful has taken place, almost holy, and these wonderful people are too wise and gracious to break the spell by asking me to explain what happened and what I am feeling.

After a few minutes, Ruth says, "Scott and Tru, I think we should let Pam and David be alone for a minute or two." She smiles and starts collecting dishes. Scott and Tru quickly get the hint and begin clearing the table and heading for the kitchen.

Pam moves next to me. I take both her hands in mine and we sit together in silence for a couple of minutes. Then an almost alien thought occurs to me: forgiveness. I need, no, I *want*, Pam's forgiveness.

The thought of asking for Pam's forgiveness jolts me for a second. I've had to say 'I'm sorry' lots of times in our marriage. But I know this is getting at something deeper, a laying bare of things that Pam isn't aware of, including things I have only thought about but not actually done.

It's hard to begin. I don't want to acknowledge the dark side of my life. I begin to realize that I have rationalized lots of moral failure. Back in Mary Mags, I honestly couldn't think of anything to repent about. Now I'm flooded with the realization that I have been the hypocrite I never wanted to be. It's humiliating to face up to the truth, to take off the mask, to be naked in front of Pam.

And then I realize that the only thing I have to lose is my pride, my pervasive, overwhelming pride. And, that my pride no longer matters, because God's love has absolutely overwhelmed my need to *be* somebody. Anybody. I don't need to protect myself, to maintain an image of being morally superior or a high achiever, a guy who's smarter, better than other people. I can just be David — warts and all.

Pam and I spend what seems like a long time going through stuff. I confess. Pam forgives — so graciously and freely that it both breaks my heart and makes me wish I had done this a long time ago. Each time I talk about something, I feel a sense of release, affirmation and healing. Both of us know that something very fundamental has changed in our lives. Pam's eyes are so full of love and compassion that I start crying again.

I know this time in the confessional has only scratched the surface of what I need to face up to and acknowledge. It will take days, weeks, years — probably a lifetime — to work through the layers of accumulated garbage and the layers of pride that cover it up.

But this amazing sense of being loved invites me in and carries me forward.

After what seems a very long time, the others return and sit down again without saying anything, just letting the sense of peace pervade the room. After a few minutes, Ruth lays her hand on my shoulder and prays for me: "Lord, fill David with your Holy Spirit. Fill him completely and give him the gifts that he needs to walk with you. And set him free from this spirit of unbelief."

Impossible as it seems, this simple prayer, which Ruth repeats several times, sets off even more dramatic reactions in me. Now the process is reversed: things leave me, as though the inflow of affirmation of Round 1 is a necessary prelude for the deliverance of Round 2. I struggle to understand what is happening. I have no conceptual framework for it and I'm missing the necessary vocabulary.

But I now see things that I have never seen before and would not believe if someone told me about them.

I see that there is a spiritual reality behind — or beyond — human experience that divides into good and evil, love and hate, freedom and bondage. The words 'Lord Jesus' have transported me into this parallel universe, this unseen world that is just beyond my reach and yet a part of my experience. And, I see that these spiritual forces are stronger than me, both the good and the evil, but that the good is more powerful than the evil. And the good is both willing and able to set me free from the evil.

Eventually, the room grows quiet again. I hear a clock ticking, some late (or early) traffic on the street. We get up from the table, say our good-byes, this time with wonderful hugs all around.

Pam and I drive back to our house. I look at the clock in the car. It's 4 am, well into a new day. Not just another day, but a New Day. In every sense of the word.

As we head out Mass Avenue, the final scene of the adventure movie unfolds.

A flood has swept away my little encampment and ended my attempt to just settle down and forget about El Dorado. It has picked me up, tumbled me over and over and finally deposited me in a new place.

I look around. I've come to rest in the middle of a lush green meadow surrounded by stunningly beautiful mountains. I hear the sound of a crystal clear stream flowing gently through the meadow. The jungle and quicksand and rocky hills and dry streambed are nowhere to be seen.

And the python is dead.

CHAPTER 42
The Bright Light of Day

Late October, Bethesda

IT'S SATURDAY AFTERNOON AND I have retreated to the study to think and process what happened last night. In the bookshelves, I spot the New Testament that I gave Pam in Africa. I pull the book down and, more or less at random, start reading the Gospel of Mark. I'm not far into it when I come across a story about Jesus that simply staggers me.

Just then, Pam sticks her head around the door.

"How are you doing, dear? I thought you could use some tea." She steps into the study, a mug of tea in each hand and a book clutched under her arm.

"Checking up to see if I'm still sane, eh?"

Pam sits down next to me on the couch and hands me a one of the mugs.

"I never thought you were."

She laughs and roughs up my hair.

I take a sip of tea.

"I'm trying to make sense out of last night. And I just read something in the Gospel of Mark that is really amazing. Listen to this:

'They went to Capernaum, and when the Sabbath came, Jesus went into the synagogue and began to teach. The people were amazed at his teaching, because he taught them as one who had authority, not as the teachers of the law.

'Just then a man in their synagogue who was possessed by an impure spirit cried out, "What do you want with us, Jesus of Nazareth? Have you come to destroy us? I know who you are— the Holy One of God!"'

"Interesting." I can tell that Pam is also trying to understand what happened last night, but doesn't entirely see the connection with Mark.

"But get this next sentence: '"Be quiet!" said Jesus sternly. "Come out of him!" The impure spirit shook *the man violently and came out of him with a shriek.*'

"What exactly are you seeing?"

"Well, it's the parallel with what happened to me last night. When Scott invited me to pray, I was just overwhelmed by the love of God. It was like the Prodigal Son coming home. I have never felt so affirmed and loved and at peace in my life. But almost immediately, I began to feel it drain away. I started to get really embarrassed about the emotional breakdown and feel foolish about losing control.

"That's when Ruth put her hand on my shoulder and started praying for me."

"What were you thinking then?"

"That she was getting carried away. The voice inside my head kept telling me not to worry, that 'nothing is going to happen' as a result of her prayer, 'nothing is going to happen'. But then the moan started."

"The moan? I thought it was much more like a scream."

Pam gives me a deadpan look and we both start laughing.

"Okay, okay. It was a scream. But it started as just a low moan. At first, I thought it was coming from somewhere in the room. As it got louder, I realized it was coming from me. When I started bouncing in the chair and pounding the table, I knew something had taken control of my body. Then I felt something leave me, and the scream stopped."

"The whole thing couldn't have lasted more than a few seconds, but it seemed like slow motion to me."

Pam looks at me as if she is checking for signs of a fever.

"Ruth seemed unfazed by it. She just kept praying – like this was all stuff she had seen before. Each time she prayed for another evil spirit, the same thing happened. The moan turned into a scream and I went through this violent shaking. Somewhere in the second or third scream, I got a vague picture of what was going on. It was like a cosmic struggle going on over my head between two forces. One was good and the other was clearly evil. Both were stronger than me. But the good was stronger than the evil.

"Crazy, huh?"

Pam sips her tea.

"Last night was a bit scary. You are the most rational and self-controlled person I know. So how does Mark relate to this?"

"I guess because it's so amazingly close to what happened to me. Ruth prayed something along the lines of 'Lord, set David free from this spirit of unbelief' or 'I tell this spirit of unbelief to leave David'. Sort of like what Jesus does in the synagogue. Except that Ruth said something like 'in Jesus' name', with an amazing sense of quiet conviction and authority.

"I think the other part of the synagogue story is that the spirit shook the man violently and then left him. That's a pretty good description of what happened to me."

"Was it scary?"

"Yeah, but probably not as you might imagine. I think most people would read the story in Mark and imagine that the guy was at least temporarily out of his mind. But I was completely alert and almost like an observer of what was going on. I remember thinking, 'if I were watching this, I wouldn't believe it.'"

Pam is quiet for a moment.

"Do you think that this was some sort of exorcism from evil spirits?"

"This may come as a shock, but I really don't know much about exorcism. Heck, I haven't even read *The Exorcist*."

We both laugh.

"I *can* tell you that it is incredibly weird to have something control your body that way, and I can think of a lot of ways to explain it other than as an exorcism. Had I been watching it happen to someone else, I would have thought it was some great emotional catharsis or a person acting out some deep fear or wish fulfillment or suffering from some deep psychological issues that are manifesting in a form of mania. Exorcism would be way down *my* list of possible explanations."

"You know, lots of people are likely to choose one or the other of those explanations, regardless of what you tell them."

I take another sip of tea and think about what she has just said.

"You're probably right. Unfortunately, those explanations don't work for me because it isn't what I experienced. But the story in Mark does. It makes sense and fits what I saw and heard. Maybe this is what God does to stubborn atheists. He just zaps them."

Pam laughs. I smile, and an imaginary headline flashes through my mind:

Rhodes Scholar Claims to Believe in Devil
Judge Orders Psychiatric Evaluation. Rhodes Trust: 'No Comment'

We head out to the kitchen to replenish our tea. Pam checks on Angela, who is having a nap, and I make certain Heather is still down the street playing with friends. We regroup in the living room.

"Someday, I will have to figure out what to tell people about last night and how. Just the experience of God's love was enough for one evening. The exorcism took me into a kind of parallel universe that is hard to explain. It's going to take some time to put the two worlds together, to find a way of living in this supernatural dimension without being totally weird in the regular world.

"And to think that all this happened because Ruth prayed for me to be set free from a spirit of unbelief. How ironic that my atheism turns out to have been a spiritual problem all of its own."

I look at Pam. Her eyes are shining and there is such a wonderful expression of love and empathy on her face. I realize how much I love her and how wonderfully special she is to me. And a deep, deep desire begins to come over me, as though something has transpired between us that has opened the door to a deeper love and greater intimacy than we have ever known.

"I'll tell you something else. The Bible is true, absolutely true. I can't tell you in what way it's true, but it's true, every word of it."

As I say this, I'm a little dumfounded. If you had asked me yesterday what I thought of the Bible, I would have said it had some redeeming qualities from a literary standpoint, but it is mediocre philosophy at best and it's largely irrelevant to the modern world and especially to my life. Today it's true. Absolutely true. And it is the most meaningful thing I have ever read.

Pam looks down at the Bible in her hands.

"I know what you mean. I read something this morning that seemed to capture what we've both been through."

'Both been through?' I suddenly remember that I was the one tagging along with Pam as she explored this Holy Spirit stuff.

"Honey, is there something that I should know?"

Pam looks a bit embarrassed.

"Last week, when I was sitting in Dumbarton Oaks, I read a book called *Aglow with the Spirit*. I came to a prayer about how to accept Jesus and then be filled with the Spirit. I prayed both prayers. I didn't feel anything other than being very peaceable and didn't think anything had happened. This morning I remembered reading that the Spirit comes when you ask. So, yes, I've been baptized in the Holy Spirit."

"Honey, that's very exciting."

I mean this sincerely, but I also realize that Pam and I are both moving very quickly out of our comfort zones. Exciting, but a little scary.

"What was it that you were reading when you came in?"

"Here, you read it for yourself and tell me what you think."

Pam hands me the Bible she carried into the room. It's open to Psalm 40.

"Where did you get this Bible?"

"It's the one my godmother gave me when I was confirmed. I don't think I've ever opened it until today."

I start reading the first few verses of Psalm 40:

"I waited patiently for the LORD; and he inclined unto me, and heard my cry.

He brought me up also out of an horrible pit, out of the miry clay, and set my feet upon a rock, and established my goings.

And he hath put a new song in my mouth, even praise unto our God: many shall see it, and fear, and shall trust in the LORD."

As I read, my eyes fill up with tears. The words seem to penetrate into my soul. 'He inclined… he heard my cry… he brought me up out of the miry clay… he set my feet on a rock… he has put a new song in my heart…'

"Were you thinking of me when you read this?"

"Yes, but also myself. I feel like I have been lifted out of the pit and set on a rock. I have a new song to sing. And, I'm really, really excited that we get to do it together."

We're both welling up as she says this.

"When I read *They Speak with Other Tongues* in Africa, I told the Lord I wanted to have the experience of the Holy Spirit. But since I was afraid that you might leave me if I did, I prayed that we might come into it at the same time. And now God has answered my prayer."

I'm rocked again. Last night seemed to come out of nowhere. The idea that its timing was the result of a two-year old prayer by my wife is hard to take in.

A little later in the afternoon, the doorbell rings. I go to the door to find Scott and Ruth on our doorstep.

"Hi! We thought we'd drop by and see how you're doing."

"Come in, come in. We're a little under slept but otherwise feeling great."

I sense that Ruth wants to make certain there hasn't been a relapse. I look at Scott.

"I've even been reading the Bible. I think I found myself in Mark."

Scott looks puzzled. "Found yourself?"

"Yeah. I could have been the guy in the synagogue in Capernaum. It's had the most profound effect on me."

I talk a bit about my reaction to reading the Bible, not just Mark 1 but Psalm 40.

Ruth listens, then says quietly.

"David, you've been through the spiritual equivalent of major surgery. You'll need some time to recover. And you need to be prepared for some spiritual warfare. Satan doesn't like to lose control of anyone, but the Lord has done an amazing work in your life."

"You mean not everyone comes to faith the way I did?"

Scott laughs.

"I've never seen anything quite like it. I am so pleased for you. But I also want to apologize for last night. I'm not one to push people into making religious commitments, and I'm sorry if you felt that I was pressuring you."

"I didn't feel pushed, Scott, I felt invited. And grateful. I've had lots of discussions and debates about religion and philosophy over the years. But this was the first time someone invited me to pray. And all it took was those two words 'Lord Jesus'. It wasn't particularly sincere. I just wanted to go home. But all that amazing stuff flowed from your invitation to pray."

"We can't stay," Ruth says warmly, "but wanted to make certain that you're doing okay. We've brought you a little gift."

She hands me a small box with a ribbon tied around it. Inside are two candle stubs.

"Those were 14 inch tapers when we sat down to dinner."

She laughs. I give her a hug, overwhelmed with gratitude for her and Scott and Tru and for the amazing thing the Lord has done for me.

"There's something else in there."

Underneath the candle stubs is a handwritten note. It says, simply, "He has called you out of darkness into his marvelous light. 1 Peter 2:9"

A lump forms in my throat, and the tears start to well up again.

"Indeed he has, Ruth, indeed he has."

Part Four

CHAPTER 43

A Different Kind of Journey

SOREN KIERKEGAARD, A 19th CENTURY Danish philosopher considered by some to be the father of Existentialism, said that '*life must be lived forward but understood backwards*'. That is, we only see the meaning of events and their role in shaping our lives in retrospect. As we live it, life is full of uncertainty and ambiguity.

Looking back, I can now see that I was on a decade long journey in two different senses. The first was an *intellectual* journey from atheism to faith. This mind and spirit journey played out in a *real-life* journey of encounters with a wide range of people from different backgrounds and locations.

As far as I was concerned, there was no particular plan to either journey. But they converged on that October night when a simple, insincere prayer unlocked a profound transformation in my understanding of the world and my place in it.

In one sense, the journey started a long time before that encounter with a Catholic priest in Salt Lake City who cared enough to challenge my atheist pride. What was significant about that encounter is that it marked the start of the journey out of atheism.

Then an Austrian art history professor introduced me to Catholic spirituality; a school teacher talked to me about death and dying; a Pentecostal evangelist listened to the voice of the Spirit and gave a student a ride on a rainy night; a geology professor talked about miracles; a Jewish friend persistently debated with me over big issues of meaning, truth and religion; and a beautiful girl from Spain gave me an idea of what Christian joy looks like.

Looming large in these memories are Clarence and Alberta. They were my life raft in a stormy sea. They showed me what a family looks like and spent countless hours discussing religion, philosophy, art, life and love. They introduced me to others who also contributed to my little pilgrimage towards meaning, including importantly, a friend of JD Salinger who sent me Newman's *Apologia*, and a farm boy turned Catholic priest in Rome.

The journey seemed to take a different path as the quest for spiritual meaning faded after Vienna. I became content to live with ambiguity, to stop being an *evangelical* atheist and just be a *reluctant* atheist.

That, of course, was not the end of the story.

A new adventure began with the Rhodes Scholarship and a love story with Pam. When I wasn't looking for meaning or purpose or God, people still kept coming into my life *as gentle reminders that life contains within it a call to transcendence*. They included Pam and her family, Heather, the Assistant Chaplain of Jesus College, the Vicar of Mary Mags, English friends who wore their faith lightly but authentically, and then, miraculously, a baby girl named Angela.

Then there were events that got my attention – the loneliness of too many nights on the road, struggles with career, coming close to dying in Africa, Angela's near fatal fall in London.

Finally, Scott and Ruth and Tru modeled Christian friendship and had the spiritual insight – and perseverance – to break through the web of spiritual deception and unbelief and tip me into the Kingdom of God.

For me, the surprising part of all these encounters is how ordered they look in retrospect. It took a lot of time and a lot of encounters, conversations, experiences and discussions for me to walk out of the darkness into the light. Few of the people involved knew each other, the locations changed constantly, and I wasn't all that aware than I was changing. In fact, I thought I hadn't changed at all. To myself, I was always the analytical, critical thinker suspicious of emotion and the kind of sentimental ideas that you find in religion.

My life changed on that October night. Profoundly. And a different kind of journey began, a journey of faith, the adventure of a walk with Jesus whose core message remains: 'Come, follow me.'

Along with the new adventure came a set of interesting and in some cases hard-won life lessons.

The discovery of the story of Jesus and the man with an unclean spirit had the effect of making the Bible the essential guidebook for this journey. I 'fell in love' with it. I read it and studied it and memorized it without trying. It became the framework through which I interpreted my experience and made my plans. I read commentaries, histories, devotional literature, even – no surprise here – books on theology.

I began re-evaluating what I wanted to do and how I wanted to live. The long-ignored sense of a calling to be a priest or pastor reasserted itself. I could easily see myself preaching to a congregation, particularly because of the way the Bible seemed to come to life in my hands. Becoming a Catholic priest was clearly out of the question given that I now had a family, but I thought (and prayed) about Episcopal/Anglican possibilities as well as other denominations.

I also felt freed from the need to 'make it' in the business world. In fact, I found my new Christian life liberating in a number of ways – from the allure of money, from the need to 'be' somebody rich or famous, from the need to sacrifice family and friends to the demands of a professional career. I decided to resign from McKinsey, to the consternation of many of my colleagues, taking my own step of faith.

We spent the first summer of our new Christian lives in North Carolina being taught and trained by Doug and Miriam. We returned to Washington, DC in the fall with no job/income but the same set of mortgage payments and school fees that we left with, minus a good chunk of the savings we had accumulated.

However, before I could get the job search organized, Scott called to say that a Christian friend (who was also a Rhodes Scholar) had a friend at the World Bank (another Rhodes Scholar) who needed some temporary help working through changes in the Bank's strategy as a result of the oil price shock after the 1973 Arab-Israeli War.

And so began an amazing two decades of work on issues of global poverty, international finance, capital raising, financial management and corporate strategy in a sophisticated multicultural organization that plays a key role in framing and promoting international cooperation. In a way, it was the El Dorado I committed to find as a Rhodes Scholar in Oxford, a place where I could make a contribution to reducing the causes of war and facilitating justice for the poor. It was a natural fit for someone of my background, and it frequently gave me a sense of being in the midst of a calling for which events, circumstances and the grace of God had prepared me.

After an initial period of five years, I left the Bank and moved to a small town in North Carolina, where I acquired a pilot's license and a small plane in order to commute back to Washington DC and elsewhere to consult for the Bank and other clients.

The reasons for this move were both positive and negative.

The positive was a desire for a more intimate Christian fellowship where I could live more consistently according to the principles that I found in Jesus' teaching. As I studied the New Testament and – especially, devotional books written by pastors, missionaries and other 'full time' Christians – I became frustrated with my own spiritual shortcomings. Despite teaching small groups and starting a lunchtime Bible study in the Bank, I was constantly aware of how ordinary – or 'sub-Christian' – my life seemed to be. Partnership with some new friends in North Carolina who were feeling the same way seemed like a God-given, Spirit-led opportunity.

The somewhat negative reason for the move was the constant collision between my increasing pietism and the culture of Washington DC. A small town in the Bible Belt seemed like a better place to raise a family (which now included our son Joshua), separated from the crassness and corruption of much of contemporary American culture and the likelihood that it was going to progressively worsen.

Nonetheless, given the need for current cash flow, I couldn't entirely get away from the Bank or big city life, as consulting on critical financial policy and strategy issues for the Bank became the way I supported the family.

We moved in the summer, and I sometimes refer to following 12 months or so as 'the Year of the Great Depression.'

The dream of an intense, deeply spiritual fellowship coupled with meaningful ministry crashed on the realities of imperfect human nature, lack of experience and cultural conflicts. It was one of the hardest times of my life, deeply disappointing and terribly disorienting. Eventually life settled down, and I still look back on the time in North Carolina as 'vintage' years of spiritual growth and deep friendship.

After three years, I decided to return to the Bank fulltime and moved the family back to DC, where I spent another ten years working on financial policy and operations for the Bank, the resolution of the 1980s international debt crisis, multilateral capital increases for the Bank Group, the economic transition in the former Soviet Union in the 1990s, aid coordination and the like, ending up in a position to influence many different areas of the Bank's operations.

In this process, I felt I had been given a wonderful opportunity to function as a peacemaker, not in the sense of negotiating the end of a war or cessation of violence, but in finding solutions to complex issues that involved deep-seated conflicts of political and economic interests, as well as social and cultural differences.

An offer to join a US investment bank in a senior capacity based in London triggered another move for us. My role in the Bank had changed, and my sense of adventure kicked in. Life is short, and while the investment-banking job came with lots of risk attached, it offered us the opportunity to live in the heart of London for a season. As it turned out, the time in London proved to be more about family than about my career.

Pam had the task of finding us a place to live, and we ended up in South Kensington, a short walk from Holy Trinity Brompton ('HTB' to its friends). The Alpha Course was just starting to spread from HTB to other churches, and Pam was drafted into helping with a conference. This eventually led to her taking on a key role in bringing the Alpha Course to the US after my investment-banking job came to an end. During this same time, Angela met the person she would eventually marry – on an Alpha Course at HTB. Our lives have remained intertwined with this amazing church and the global Christian community that it has fostered.

The point of telling these stories is that 'following Jesus' turned out to be a very different kind of life than what I imagined (or feared) when I was in Vienna. My 'call' was not to the priesthood, but to be engaged in the world of finance and business. It wasn't necessarily what I wanted, and it was not what I expected. But I understood that the heart of the matter was to be available and ready to go where Jesus seemed to be leading me, whether through circumstances, desire, intuition, fit with my personality/ background, or the counsel of others.

In other words, it is a matter of faithfulness, often in the face of uncertainty and with no guarantees of success. In the end, the Christian life is not about my interests but Christ's, whatever the consequences for me. My 'call', and I think a key part of every Christian calling, is to be in the midst of the world, in the marketplace and not just the cloister, ready to have our fur rubbed off like the Velveteen Rabbit.

I also believe that conflict is part of the deal. If you are looking for a stress-free, conflict-free life, don't try to follow Jesus. Conflict will find you at work, at home, in large churches, and in small group fellowships, in small towns. That's why peacemakers are so important and valued. Peacemaking is hard work and it requires deep-seated character traits (humility, compassion, absence of self interest, purity of motive, etc.) and lots of commitment.

Moreover, it's okay to fall short spiritually. Piety is a good thing, but the wrong kind of pietism may drive a person out of the place of calling, as it did with me for a season. The Bible is the story of imperfect people in the hands of a gracious God. It is also a story of people in transition, on the move from one place or condition to another. When things are nice and stable and predictable and secure, we don't do a lot of searching for meaning and truth. It's in the Exodus moments of our lives that the cosmic yearning is awakened and we discover the One who calls.

Finally, I have tried to keep in mind that just being an *influence* may be most or all of the evangelism I do. My own story is about people along the way who influenced me in ways that caused me to think differently about my atheism, to become interested in the Christian faith, to get some sense of who Jesus is and his call to come and follow him. They shared their lives and prayed for me, and became my friends. In the end, their stories became part of my story.

My hope – and prayer – is that my story might become part of your story.

CHAPTER 44

From Darkness to Light

"I am sending you to them to open their eyes and turn them from darkness to light, and from the power of Satan to God..."

JESUS TO SAUL OF TARSUS,
ON THE DAMASCUS ROAD

SO WHAT ABOUT THAT BIG night in October? What part of that strange physical/spiritual experience survived contact with the world of international finance and politics?

The short answer is: *all of it.* Let me explain.

First of all, what happened to me was both radical and supernatural. It was radical in that my whole worldview changed. It was supernatural in that it resulted from a work of the Spirit of God to turn me from darkness to light and from the power of Satan to God. It was – and I mean this quite literally – a miracle.

Whether you believe in miracles or not has everything to do with your *worldview*, i.e., the presuppositions that you use to define truth, set the boundaries of knowledge and interpret experience.

As an atheist, I thought of myself as a modern, thoroughly rational and scientific sort of guy. I also thought I was pretty good at cutting the ground out from under religious arguments and religious people. I restricted true knowledge to propositions that could be verified empirically, using essentially scientific principles. More importantly, I was convinced that the physical world is *all that there is and all that we can know.* Everything else was illusion, self-deception or myth. Including miracles.

On that October night, I saw something else. I saw something beyond the material world, something transcendent and 'spiritual.' This transcendent way of seeing and thinking is at the heart of the Christian experience. In the Christian paradigm, the physical world that we know and understand scientifically, that part of reality that we can see and feel and touch, is not self-originating or simply 'accidental'. Rather, it is created within, is part of, and is surrounded by, the non-material world. It does not exist on its own. Nor is it the most important reality.

Scientific inquiry and communication work because scientists – atheists and religious believers alike – make a small number of critical assumptions about what we know and how we know it, in particular, that the physical universe is all there is, that we can accurately detect and measure it using our senses, and that it operates according to cause and effect principles with very high levels of confidence. These assumptions are so widely accepted and relied upon that even scientists sometimes forget the limits of what they can say as scientists. For example, a statement like, 'the physical universe is all there is' is not empirically verifiable. You would need to be outside of the universe in order to know that. Nor is a statement like 'the physical universe is all that we can *know*'.

The same is true, of course, for my former atheist worldview. It 'piggy backed' on the scientific paradigm by *presuming* that the material world is all that is and all that we can know. Using this convenient but inadequate framework, I then proceeded to evaluate religious belief and experience inaptly and – in many respects – ineptly. In contrast, I now see that the overall context of human knowledge is much more complex, dramatic and beautiful than I ever imagined in my atheist days. *Imprisoned by my own atheist ideology*, I closed my mind to the idea of God and it took a series of wonderfully patient people and some jarring encounters with reality to re-open it.

Second, I think the most important thing I discovered through this intellectual revolution is that – consciously or unconsciously – *we all choose our worldview*. And if we choose a worldview, rather than have it inevitably thrust upon us by science or philosophy, then it is critical to choose a good one.

Like love and beauty, life's meaning and purpose are anchored in our subjective experience of the external world. Intuition often tells us far deeper things than reason alone. Or, as Pascal said, '*The heart has its reasons about which reason has no clue*' (my translation). We need to trust our intuition in things of the heart, and not allow it to be deconstructed and discredited by explanations anchored in undisclosed and unexamined assumptions about what we can know and how we know it.

To that end, I find the Judeo-Christian (or 'Biblical') view of God, the problem of evil and its remedy, God's activity in creation, redemption and – ultimately – the renewal of all things by his Spirit through the Messiah to be a compelling master narrative. My experience of redemption from my own failures, mistakes and wrong choices locks into this narrative like a tiny piece in a very large and complex puzzle.

Third, this shift in worldview was so sudden and radical that it seems fitting to describe it as being *born again*, a change in my way of seeing, understanding, believing and *being*. It is radical language that points to a radical change in the way I *see* things, as radical as going from deep darkness into the bright light of day. Or as John Newton put it in his hymn *Amazing Grace*, "I once was blind but now I see." The most amazing part for me is that this shift in belief or perception about God and his enemies was not produced by a 'leap of faith', an abandonment of reason, or a lapse in rationality but by a simple prayer.

Christianity is, of course, a religion based on miracles, one miracle in particular: the resurrection of Jesus. Moreover, faith in Jesus' resurrection that results in seeing him as the Son of God is itself a miracle, a work of the Holy Spirit in the heart of the believer. As the Apostle Paul says, "no one can say, 'Jesus is Lord' except by the Holy Spirit."

Not everyone who becomes a Christian does so in quite the dramatic and visible way that I did. But being born again (or 'born from above') is always a miracle, and the Christian life operates in both the spiritual (or 'supernatural') world and the physical/material (i.e., 'natural') world.

Fourth, a Christian at prayer is a Christian in touch with this supernatural dimension of life, and prayer is the main means by which Christians participate in the battle between good and evil. In my experience, evil abounds in the world, and people are generally unaware of how the battle between God and his enemies is playing out in their lives. The difference for Christians is that they have been 'tipped off' about what is going on behind the scenes, have *authority* over the powers of darkness, and are thus in a position to pray for themselves, for the situations they find themselves in, and most importantly, for the people they are with – Christian or not. Prayer is what we do.

Prayer is thus the way I make sense of my experience that October night. I don't know why my journey towards Christ culminated in a dramatic deliverance from the forces of evil. I only know that it happened and that it gave me insight and capacity to do the same for others.

My professional life thus became a combination of pursuing excellence in problem solving/peace making and engaging in unseen intercessory prayer for anyone or anything where I discerned that spiritual evil might be at work.

I don't think you could have designed a less likely or more unacceptable way for me to become a Christian. After all, I wasn't some guy in dirty clothes stumbling around the streets of Washington DC with a catatonic look in his eye. I might have made it into Church eventually along the path of a proper Anglican. But the idea that evil could find its source in a spiritual personality who was seeking to displace God in the minds and affections of human beings was preposterous. Both God and the devil seemed to me to be projections of ignorant people onto events and behaviors that they couldn't – or didn't want to – understand.

Until it happened to me.

Psalm 37 talks about the steps of a person 'being ordered by the Lord.' My journey didn't seem particularly orderly at the time. But looking back it does. There were so many places where I could have gotten lost, made fatal mistakes, or ruined my life. I could have continued down the hardline atheist path and become a political revolutionary. I could have become a bitter social critic. Or a drug addict. Or a suicide. I could have died on the plains of Africa.

But none of these things happened. Instead, my steps were ordered, my way protected, until I found my way home.

Ultimately, my story is a story of the *unmerited favor* of God, his amazing grace that pursues his enemies until they surrender to his loving embrace. And that's why it's a Biblical story. I find myself in the story of the Prodigal Son, in the call of Abraham, in Jacob's wrestling match with the

Lord, in Israel's wandering in the wilderness, in dozens of other characters in the Bible whose stories we know because the Lord called them to himself and took action to see that they didn't miss the call.

I rejected God as a teenager, and that should have been the end of it. But it wasn't. The God of the Bible pursued, protected, called, wooed and finally delivered me from my self-imposed Egyptian bondage to atheism.

Once again, a sense of irony overtakes me. My confession of faith as an atheist in a Salt Lake City parking lot came with a lot of conviction. But that confession simply preceded a time of testing of those convictions. I got to look into the abyss of meaninglessness and see where my intellectual arrogance – or 'pride', as the priest called it – was leading me.

Even more ironically, where pride increased, grace seemed to increase all the more.

In the end, I needed to pray – fitfully, imperfectly and almost against my better judgment. But two words were all it took to unlock this amazing transformation of worldview – *Lord Jesus*. As the Apostle Paul puts it in his letter to the Christians in Rome, 'if you confess with your mouth that Jesus is Lord and believe in your heart that God raised him from the dead, you will be saved.'

However, I wouldn't describe my experience as a big act of faith. It was indirect, and *faith followed the action* of saying the words. Words have power.

Words create reality in our lives, good or bad. At the time, I thought my confession as an atheist was liberating, affirming and empowering. As it turns out, the half-hearted confession of 'Lord Jesus' unleashed a far, far greater sense of affirmation and set me free in ways I couldn't imagine beforehand.

I think CS Lewis summarizes this revolution in worldview, which he himself experienced, incredibly well: "I believe in Christianity as I believe that the sun has risen: not only because I see it, but because by it I see everything else."

The Rhodes Scholarship and the opportunity to study at Oxford was one of the more amazing manifestations of the unmerited favor of God in my life. At first, Oxford was the secular El Dorado of my Utah dreams, the place where religion no longer had a place. Years later, I now see my Oxford experience as an integral part of the story of a firebrand young atheist ultimately transformed 'in the twinkling of an eye' into a follower of Christ.

And, in my case at least, the University's motto is apt indeed:

Dominus Illuminatio Mea – the Lord is my light.

About the Author

David Bock grew up in Eastern Idaho. He studied philosophy as an undergraduate – including two years at the University of Vienna – and then attended Oxford University as a Rhodes Scholar. He has a BA degree in philosophy from the University of Washington and a graduate degree in economics from Oxford University.

After Oxford, David joined McKinsey & Company, serving clients in Europe, Africa and the US. He then worked as an executive of the World Bank in Washington DC for the better part of two decades with responsibilities in financial policy and strategy, capital raising and lending operations. Subsequently, he joined a major investment bank in London as a managing director with responsibility for emerging markets corporate finance.

David returned to the US in the mid-90s as a private equity investor, entrepreneur and financial executive. He now serves on the boards of several investment management companies and nonprofit organizations.

David and his wife Pam reside in Austin, Texas.

Made in the USA
Charleston, SC
28 July 2016